500 SERMON OUTLINES

Bible Truths

John Ritchie

Kregel
Academic & Professional

500 Sermon Outlines on Bible Truths

by John Ritchie

Published in 1987 by Kregel Publications, a division of Kregel, Inc., P.O. Box 2607, Grand Rapids, MI 49501.

Library of Congress Cataloging-in-Publication Data
Ritchie, John, 1853–1930.
500 sermon outlines on basic Bible truths / by John Ritchie.
 p. cm.
 Reprint. Originally published: Five Hundred Bible Subjects. Kilmarnock: J. Ritchie, 1926.
 1. Bible—Outlines, syllabi, etc. I. Title. II. Title: Five Hundred Bible Subjects.
BS418.R57   1987   251'.02   86-27541

ISBN 0-8254-3582-x

Printed in the United States of America

06 07 / 5 4 3 2

CONTENTS

PUBLISHER'S PREFACE

"Preach the Word" was the admonition that Paul gave to the young preacher, Timothy (2 Tim. 4:2). What was so essential 2000 years ago is still necessary today. To "preach the Word" is to expound Scripture truths with clarity and conviction.

The *John Ritchie Sermon Outline* series has helped many to preach effectively since they were first published. Based on Scripture portions, these outlines bring out truths that change lives and minister to present needs. These aids are not intended to diminish a personal, prayerful study of the Bible. Rather, they will encourage it by giving insights to those who preach or teach God's truths.

These brief sermon outlines will enlighten, instruct and give direction to the believer as he walks the path marked out in the Word. They will also refresh and strengthen the inner man in his desire to better know God's word.

For the busy preacher or lay person who needs stimulating ideas for a dynamic preaching or teaching ministry, these sermon outlines will be most beneficial.

HOW TO READ AND STUDY
THE WORD OF GOD

The Bible is God's own Book, His divine and perfect Revelation, His living Voice speaking unto men, in all ages. It should be read prayerfully, listened to reverently, received believingly, obeyed implicitly. Its central object is Christ; its Teacher, the Holy Spirit; its design, man's blessing; its end, the glory of God. It is the instrument of regeneration, the means of sanctification, the channel of edification to the believer. It gives light upon all his path, regulates all his relationships, and gives counsel for all his behavior in the family, the church, and the world. It should be dealt with daily, personally, prayerfully, purposely, perseveringly, in the presence of God, for the soul's individual need. It is bread to feed, light to search, water to cleanse; the secret of growth, the source of strength, the shield of preservation, the sword of victory.

Read it regularly, connectedly, consecutively. Give your heart and mind the whole field of Scripture; Christ in type and prophecy in the Old Testament; Christ on earth, in life, in death, and in glory in the New Testament. The Bible is from God. It is divinely inspired, has been miraculously guarded, is of supreme authority, all-sufficient, and eternal, the standard of doctrine, a channel of blessing, the rule of life, the final appeal on all God's things in all ages.

Nothing needs to be added to it because nothing is missing; nothing taken from it because nothing is superfluous. Like its Author, it is divine, unchanging, eternal. Its writers were men, but their words were the words of the Holy Spirit (2 Peter 1:21; 2 Sam. 13:2). It was accepted as it existed; was read, used, and spoken of as "the Word of God" (Mark 7:13), "the Scripture" which cannot be broken (John 10:35) by the Lord Jesus. It is declared that He "knew all men" (John 2:24), and had "all things" given into His hand (John 3:35), of whom His own disciples confessed, "now we are sure that thou knowest all things" (John 16:30) — a glory which some deny Him. Would He have put His imprimatur upon a book, accepting its various divisions as they stood (Luke 24:43-44), calling it the "Scriptures," opening His disciples' understanding that they might understand these Scriptures, and sending the Spirit to teach and guide them into "all the truth" therein contained, had He believed, as some now would fain persuade us, that the Book is a combination of truth and error, of divine revelation and human legend? The Bible carries its own credentials. It causes its voice to be heard. Its light convicts, its warnings alarm, its grace converts the soul. It shows man, reveals God, testifies of Christ. It is the instrument in conversion, the means of instruction, the power for edification. It teaches the babe, guides the youth, and fully furnishes "the man of God" unto all good works.

All God's mighty men have been readers, students, lovers of the Book. Charles H. Spurgeon says: "The Word, the simple, pure, infallible Word of God we must live upon, if we are to become strong against error and tenacious of truth." Robert C. Chapman writes: "Meditation on the Word of God is the chief means of our growth in grace. It is a thriving soul that finds the Book of God growing more and more precious." J. Nelson Darby testifies — "My joy, my comfort, my food, my strength for near thirty years has been the Scriptures received implicitly as the Word of God. In the beginning of that period I was put through the deepest exercise on that point. Should heaven and earth, the visible church, and man himself crumble into nonentity, I would, through grace since that epoch, hold to the Word as an unbreakable link between my soul and God."

Read the Word *daily.* Set apart a fixed time for the daily reading of the Word. When left to be read at any time it is frequently not read at all. Keep to your set time, do not allow trivial engagements, social functions, or business calls to deprive you of it. God and the soul first, other things fall into their proper places after.

Read the Word *prayerfully.* In prayer you speak to God: through the Word God speaks to you. While your eyes rest on the sacred page, let your heart be lifted up to God with the prayer that the eye of faith may be opened to "behold wondrous things" out of His law (Ps. 119:18). Remember that the Spirit of God is your Teacher, that He, by whose inspiration these words of God were written, alone can unfold their spiritual meaning to your understanding and your heart (1 Cor. 2:10-14), and make them strength and comfort to your soul. When you discover some fresh aspect of truth, when you dig out some hitherto unknown treasure, when some new ray of heaven's light enters your heart, meditate on it, speak to God about it, praise Him for it, ask Him to make it your soul's personal possession, to make it good to you experimentally.

George Müeller, of Bristol, says: "It is a common temptation of Satan to make us give up the reading of the Word and prayer when our enjoyment is gone, as if it were of no use to read the Scriptures when we do not enjoy them and as if it were of no use to pray when we have no spirit of prayer. The truth is that, in order to enjoy the Word, we ought to continue to read it. The way to obtain a spirit of prayer is to continue praying for the less we read it and the less we pray, the less we desire to pray."

Helps to the study of the Bible are not to be despised, nor ought they to be neglected. We may surely profit through the toils of others who have given their time and talents to the textual criticism, careful translation, and microscopic examination of the sacred Word. His servants become helpers one of another. But let the Book of books, the inspired, eternal Word of the living God have the chief and honored place. Let it be THE Book, the supreme authority, and all else but as helps to the discovery of its holy treasures, hewers of wood, and drawers of water to the sacred volume which they seek to serve. Have a good *reference Bible*, with readable type and margin sufficient for notes and jottings; one good enough to last a number of years of hard wear, for it is not good to change your Bible often. A *revised* or other *translation*, a complete and trustworthy *concordance* to the Bible, and a reliable *Bible dictionary* are useful and now easily acquired helps in the study of the sacred Word. These, with expositions of truths by gifted and divinely-taught ministers of the Word, are to be received with thanksgiving and used with wisdom, always in leading you to the Word to dig there for yourselves, never to take its place, or to be read as a lesson book to be repeated to others, without having been proved or personally experienced in your own souls. *Commentaries*, as a rule, are theological and dry; many of them muddy, some quite erroneous, and generally even when sound, cold-blooded, with little in them to enrich the soul, exercise the conscience, or lead the heart out to God. The Word of God itself, under the teaching of the Spirit, opens its secret treasures to the waiting heart, which in patient, diligent, and continuous study of its sacred pages, seeks to become acquainted with the will of God to do it, and with the ways of the Lord to walk in them. Regular and systematic study of the Word, day-by-day, and every day, gathering here a little and there a little, treasuring, husbanding, and using what we gather, is the slow but sure and only way of becoming acquainted with the whole truth of God.

Methods of study must be largely left to the tastes, the capabilities, and the conveniences of the individual. What suits one well does not lend itself to another. Clearly there must be some method or many methods adopted; random reading profits little. The Word should be studied systematically, consecutively, topically. The character, scope, subject, and purpose of a book; the outlines, context, setting, subject, occasion, date, and keywords sought for and grasped; then its teaching will be understood, its doctrinal, dispensational, and practical parts distinguished, and its application made plain; "rightly dividing the Word of truth" (2 Tim. 2:16), as the apostle commands. Error is often truth distorted, wrenched from its connection, and presented from one side apart from the countertruth needed for its balance.

Searching the Scriptures, tracing a word, a subject through them, as a dog scents (for such is the meaning of the word "search the Scriptures" in John 5:39), is one method. "Searching the Scriptures" — examining them closely, scrutinizing, and comparing them, as the Bereans did (Acts 17:12), is equally important for the accurate study of the Word. Thus acquainted with the truths of Scripture, having them dwelling richly in the mind and heart, kept there in freshness by the Holy Spirit who indwells the saint (2 Tim. 1:13-14), they will be brought to remembrance, and wisdom given to utter them by that same Spirit (1 Cor. 2:13-14), in due season with blessing to others.

May the Book of God, the written Word, in which the Living Word is unveiled, become increasingly precious unto and be unceasingly used by all the people of God.

"A glory gilds the sacred page,
Majestic like the sun;
It gives a light to every age,
It gives, but borrows none."

BASIC TRUTHS
OF THE GOSPEL

1   Regeneration

A New Life from God, an Inward Working in the Soul

Its Necessity (John 3:7; Gal. 6:15; Eph. 2:2)
Its Nature (John 3:5; 2 Cor. 5:17; Eph. 2:10; 4:24)
Its Agent (John 3:8; 6:63; 2 Cor. 3:6; Titus 3:5)
Its Instrument (1 Peter 1:23; James 1:18; John 5:24)
Its Means (1 John 5:1; Gal. 3:26; John 1:12-13)
Its Fruits (1 John 3:9; Rom. 6:22; 1 John 3:10)
Its Manifestation (1 John 5:1-2; 1 John 3:16)

2   Conversion

A New Attitude Toward God, an Outward Change in the Life

The Need (Matt. 18:3; Acts 3:19; Isa. 53:6)
The Act (1 Thess. 1:9; 1 Peter 2:24; Acts 26:18)
The Motive (Acts 11:21; Hosea 14:8; Phil. 3:8)
The Hindrances (Acts 28:27; 13:8; John 6:66)

3   Justification

A New State before God, a Forensic Term

The Sinner's State (Rom. 3:10; Isa. 64:6; Rom. 3:9)
God, the Justifier (Rom. 8:33; 4:25)
Christ's Death, the Procuring Cause (1 Peter 3:18)
Grace, the Spring (Rom. 3:24; Gal. 2:16-24)
Faith, the Principle (Rom. 5:1; Acts 13:39)
Resurrection, the Witness (Rom. 4:25; 5:18)
Works, the Evidence (James 2:26; Titus 3:8)

4   Redemption

The Word means "to buy back" and set free
There is a Redemption by Blood and by Power

Man's Ruin (Isa. 52:3; John 8:34; Rom. 6:20)
Man's Helplessness (Ps. 49:7; Micah 6:7)
A Redeemer Provided (Job 33:24; Ps. 111:9)
Redemption by Blood (Eph. 1:7; Acts 20:28; Heb. 9:12)
Redemption by Power (Eph. 1:13-14; 4:30; Rom. 8:23)
Redemption from Iniquity (Titus 2:14; 1 Peter 1:18)
Redemption from the Curse (Gal. 3:13; Ps. 103:4)
Redemption of the Body (Rom. 8:23; Phil. 3:20)

5   Salvation

Threefold—Past, Present, Future

Past—From Sin's Penalty (Rom. 1:16; Acts 28:18; Acts 16:31; Rom. 10:10; 1 Cor. 15:2; 2 Tim. 1:9)
Present—From Sin's Power (Heb. 7:25; Rom. 5:9; James 1:23; 1 Tim. 4:6; Phil. 2:12)
Future—From Sin's Presence (Rom. 13:11; Heb. 9:28; Phil. 3:20; 1 Thess. 5:8)
The *First* is immediate, secured by Christ's *Death*
The *Second* is continuous by Christ's *Life*
The *Third* is prospective at Christ's *Coming*

6   Judgment

In Various Aspects

Judgment of the Sinner, Predicted (Heb. 9:27; Eccl. 11:9; 2 Peter 2:2-4; Heb. 10:27)

Judgment of the Believer, Past (John 5:24; Rom. 8:1; 8:23-24; Gal. 2:20)

Judgment of the Servant, Future (2 Cor. 5:10; Rev. 22:12; Col. 3:24-25; 1 Cor. 4:1-5)

There is no such thing as a General Judgment taught in the Scriptures.

7   Sanctification

The word means "to set apart," "to separate"

The Sanctification of Believers (1 Cor. 1:2; 2 Thess. 2:13; 1 Peter 1:3)

1. *Perfect* and *Once* for All—The Work of the Cross, the result of the Sacrifice of Christ (1 Cor. 6:2; Acts 20:32; 26:18; Heb. 2:11)

2. *Progressive* and *Continuous*—The Work of the Spirit through the Word in the believer (1 Thess. 5:23; John 17:17)

Types and Illustrations—The Sabbath sanctified (Gen. 2:3; The First Born "set apart" (Exod. 13:2); The Brazen Altar, the Holy Garments (Exod. 29:44; 28:2) and the Holy Mount (2 Peter 1:18) accounted "sacred" or "holy," not intrinsically, but "set apart" by the presence and for the service of God.

8 Perfection

The words "Perfect" and "Perfection" represent several
Greek words having different meanings.

1. *Teleois*, meaning "accomplished, complete," which
   occurs in Matthew 5:48 as applied to God, in Rom.
   10:2 to His "will," in 1 John 4:17 to His love, and is rendered
   "full age" in Heb. 5:14, "full grown" in Heb. 5:14.
2. *Pleero*, meaning "full," rendered "perfect" in Rev. 3:2;
   "complete," Col. 3:10; and "full" in 1 John 1:4.
3. *Katarizo*, meaning "thoroughly adjusted," as in
   "mending nets" (Mark 1:19). It is translated "perfectly
   joined together" (1 Cor. 1:10); "restore" (Gal. 6:1). By
   carefully distinguishing these words many of the diffi-
   culties regarding this subject are removed.

Absolutely, perfection is in God alone (Job 37:16)
Relatively, it is said to be of men (Job 1:8; Ps. 36:17)
1. Perfection of God (Matt. 5:48; Rom. 12:2; 2 Sam. 23:11)
2. Perfection of Christ (Heb. 2:10; 12:2)
3. Perfect Sacrifice (Heb. 10:11-14; 7:28)
4. Perfect Conscience (Heb. 10:2-14; John 17:10)
5. Perfection in Practice (Matt. 5:48; 2 Cor. 13:11)
6. Perfection in Growth (Heb. 5:14; Phil. 3:15)
"Sinlessness," "perfection" of the creature, is an error
(see 1 John 1:8).

9 Assurance

Certainty, not Doubt, is the Christian's normal condition

What Believers *Are* (1 Cor. 1:18; 1 John 2:12)
What Believers *Know* (1 John 3:14, 24; 5:11, 19)
What Believers *Have* (Eph. 1:7; 5:1; John 3:14)
What Believers *Expect* (1 John 3:2; 1 Thess. 4:16)

10   Sonship

The word *Teknon* means "begotten ones," and occurs in John 1:12; 11:52; Rom. 8:16-17; Phil. 2:15; 1 John 3:1-2

The word *Whyos* means "sons," and occurs in Gal. 3:26; 4:6-7; Rom. 8:14-19; Heb. 12:5, 7-8

The Origin of Sonship (Gal. 3:26; 1 John 5:1)
The Spirit of Sonship (Gal. 4:6-7; Rom. 8:14)
The Place of Sonship (John 8:35; Gal. 4:5)
The Manifestation of Sonship (Rom. 8:19-29)

11   Rest

There are at least three words translated "Rest"
in the New Testament

1. *Anapausis*—"an up rest," as in Matt. 11:28
2. *Katapausis*—"a down rest," as in Heb. 4:4
3. *Sabbatismos*—"a Sabbath rest," as in Heb. 4:9
Rest for the Sinner (Matt. 11:28)—At the Cross
Rest for the Saint (Matt. 11:29)—In Subjection
Rest in the Lord (Ps. 36:7)—In Confidence
Rest with the Lord (2 Thess. 1:7)—In Glory
Rest that Remains (Heb. 4:9)—Eternal

12   Life

The Sinner's State (Eph. 2:1; Eph. 4:18; John 6:53)
The Source of Life (John 5:26; Ps. 36:9)
The Life Manifested (1 John 1:4; John 1:4)
The Life Laid Down (John 10:15; John 12:24)
The Life Imparted (John 10:10; 20:31; Rom. 6:23)
The Life Possessed (John 3:36; 1 John 5:12-13)
The Life Exhibited (2 Cor. 4:10; Gal. 2:20)
The Life in Fruition (Titus 1:2; Jude 21; Rom. 6:22)

FUNDAMENTAL TRUTHS
OF THE FAITH

13   The Triune God

Read Matthew 28:18; 2 Corinthians 13:14
The Father (Eph. 4:6; Rom. 11:36; Rom. 9:5)
The Son (John 5:20; 10:20; 17:5; Matt. 11:27)
The Holy Spirit (John 14:26; 15:26; 16:7)
Godhead ascribed to each (Rom. 1:20; Heb. 1:8)

14   Trinity Acting in Unity

In Creation (Gen. 1:1, with John 1:4; Job 26:13)
In Incarnation (John 3:16; Heb. 10:5; Luke 1:35)
In Redemption (Heb. 9:14; 1 Peter 3:18; Gal. 2:20)
In Salvation (Luke 15:4, 8, 22; Eph. 1:4, 7, 13)
In Communion (Eph. 2:18; Rom. 8:27; 2 Cor. 13:14)
In Glory (Rev. 1:4-5; Phil. 3:21; Jude 23)

15   The Work of God, the Father

Election of the Saints (Eph. 1:3)
Giver of the Son (John 3:16)
Author of Incarnation (Gal. 4:4)
Anointing for Service (Acts 10:38)
Bruising in Death (Isa. 53:6-11)
Active in Resurrection (Rom. 6:4)
Sealer of Salvation (2 Cor. 1:21-22)

16   The Eternal Godhead

The Eternal God (Deut. 33:27; Isa. 57:15)
The Eternal Son (John 1:1; Micah 5:2)
The Eternal Spirit (Heb. 9:14; Gen. 1:2; Job 26:13)

17   Three Great Truths

Concerning Christ in John, chapter 1, verse 1

His Eternity—"In the *beginning* was the Word"
His Personality—"The Word was *with* God"
His Divinity—"The Word *was* God"

18   Son of God

In the Eternal Past (John 8:58; 1:30; 17:5)
As Given to the World (John 3:16; Rom. 8:3)
As Born of the Virgin (Luke 1:35; John 1:14)
As Owned of the Father (Matt. 3:17; Luke 9:35)
As Confessed by Men (Matt. 16:16; Acts 9:20)
As Raised from the Dead (Rom. 1:4; Heb. 1:1)

19   The Son of Man

A Title only used by the Lord concerning Himself, never by His disciples in speaking to or of Him. It designates His true Manhood, as distinguished from the "sons of men," whose humanity is "fallen."

In Service and Suffering (Matt. 11:19; Luke 9:56)
Coming to Save (Luke 19:10; John 6:27)
Suffering unto Death (Luke 9:22; 24:7)
A Sacrifice for Sin (John 3:14; 12:34)
Risen from the Dead (Matt. 17:9; 12:32)
Glorified in Heaven (Acts 7:56; Rev. 1:13)
Coming in Judgment (Matt. 24:17; 25:31)

20   The Divine Sonship of Christ

A Sevenfold Testimony

Jesus proclaimed it (Matt. 26:63)
The Father affirmed it (Matt. 3:17)
The Resurrection declared it (Rom. 1:4)
Paul preached it (Acts 9:20)
Peter confessed it (Matt. 16:16)
Demons acknowledged it (Mark 3:11)
Disciples believed it (Matt. 14:33)

21   The Incarnation

The Word became flesh (John 1:14; 1 Tim. 3:16)
Partook of flesh and blood (Heb. 2:14-17; 5:7)
Born of a woman (Gal. 4:4, with Luke 1:30-35)
Took the form of a servant (Phil. 2:7; Luke 22:27)
In the likeness of sinful flesh (Rom. 8:3; 1 Peter 3:18)
The Holy One of God (Mark 1:24; Acts 3:14)
The Image of His Person (Heb. 1:2; John 1:18)

22   The Deity of Christ

Proclaimed by the Father (Matt. 1:23; John 1:1)
Claimed by the Son (John 10:30; John 5:21; Rev. 1:8)
Witnessed by the Spirit (Heb. 1:8; 1 Peter 3:15)
Owned by Angels (Heb. 1:6; Rev. 5:11-12)
Confessed by Saints (John 20:28; Rom. 9:5)
Feared by Demons (Mark 5:7; James 2:19)
Manifested by His Works (Luke 7:20; John 5:36)

23   The Resurrection of Christ

Attributed to the Father (Rom. 6:4; Col. 2:12)
Attributed to the Son (John 10:18; Luke 24:6-7)
Attributed to the Spirit (1 Peter 3:18; Rom. 8:11)

24 The Perfect Sacrifice of Christ

Offered once for all upon the Cross

It was an Expiation (Rom. 8:3; Gal. 1:4)
It was a Death Sentence (Gal. 3:13; 2 Cor. 5:23)
It was for a Propitiation (Rom. 3:23; 1 John 2:2)
It was a Purchase (1 Cor. 6:20; Acts 20:28)
It was a Peacemaking (Col. 1:20; Isa. 53:5)

25 Four Aspects of Resurrection

The Seal of a Finished Work (Acts 13:29-30)
The Sign of a Glorious Triumph (Heb. 2:14; Eph. 4:8)
The Pledge of a Coming Resurrection (1 Cor. 15:20-22)
The Certainty of a Future Judgment (Acts 17:31)

26 The Present Ministry of Christ

In Heaven for His Saints

As their Shepherd (Heb. 13:20)—Guiding
As their High Priest (Heb. 4:14, with 2:17)—Succoring
As their Advocate (1 John 2:2)—Interceding
As their Lord (Acts 2:36)—Ruling

27 The Coming of the Lord

For His Saints

The Lord's Promise (John 14:3; Rev. 22:7, 12, 20)
A Personal Return (Acts 1:11; Rev. 22:16)
Descends to the Air (1 Thess. 4:16)
The Dead in Christ Rise (1 Thess. 4:16; 1 Cor. 15:52)
The Living are Changed (1 Thess. 4:17; 1 Cor. 15:51)
Caught up Together (1 Thess. 4:17; 2 Thess. 2:1)
With, and Like the Lord (1 Thess. 4:17)

28   The Appearing of the Lord

With His Saints

In Majesty and Power (2 Thess. 1:7; Rev. 19:11)
In Manifested Glory (Matt. 24:30; Titus 2:12)
With all His Saints (Col. 3:4; Rom. 8:19)
To Judge His Enemies (Jude 15; Acts 17:31)
To Punish Grace Despisers (2 Thess. 1:9; Acts 13:41)
To Destroy Antichrist (2 Thess. 2:8; Rev. 19:20)
To Deliver Creation (Rom. 8:21; Isa. 11:6)

29   The Judgment of the Dead

The Judgment Throne (Rev. 20:2; Ps. 89:14)
The Seated Judge (John 5:27; Ps. 9:4)
The Resurrected Culprits (John 5:28-29; Rev. 20:12)
The Opened Books (Rev. 20:12; Eccl. 12:14)
The Final Sentence (Rev. 20:14; 21:8)

30   The Punishment of the Wicked

Foretold by Patriarchs (Deut. 32:22; Job 36:18)
Warned of by Prophets (Ps. 9:17; Isa. 5:14; 14:9)
Described by the Lord (Matt. 25:46; Mark 9:47)
Taught by Apostles (2 Peter 2:9; Heb. 10:29)
Unveiled in Revelation (Rev. 14:10; 20:14-15)
Denied by Scoffers (2 Peter 3:4; Jude 18)

31   The Creation of Man

The Work of God (Gen. 1:26-27; 2:7)
In His Image (Gen. 1:27; 5:1; Eccl. 7:29; James 3:9)
Spirit, Soul, and Body (Gen. 2:7; 1 Thess. 5:23)
The Unity of Mankind (Acts 17:26; Gen. 9:16)
Man's Eternal Existence (John 5:28-29; Rev. 20:12)

32   The Fall and Its Consequences

Adam's Personal Fall (Gen. 2:17; 3:7-8)
The Penal Consequences (Rom. 5:12-17; 1 Cor. 15:22)
The Inherited Nature (Eph. 2:3; Ps. 51:5)
The Total Depravity (Rom. 3:9-18; 5:19-20)
The Need of Regeneration (Job 14:4; John 3:3)

33   The Personality of the Spirit

Described by the Lord Jesus (John 14:16-17; 15:26)
Not an Influence, but a Person (Acts 5:9; Matt. 12:31-33)
His Words and Works (Acts 8:29, 39; 13:2-4; 16:6)
His Attributes and Character (1 Cor. 2:10; 2 Peter 1:21)
Sent and Come (John 15:26; Acts 2:1-4; 5:32)
Received and Rejected (Acts 10:44; Eph. 1:13; Acts 7:51)

34   The Designations of the Spirit

The Comforter, Paraclete, Helper (John 14:26)
The Searcher, Revealer, Teacher (1 Cor. 2:10-14)
The Strengthener, Indweller, Guide (Eph. 3:16)

35   The Work of the Spirit

In the World (John 16:8-11; 1 Peter 1:12; 1 Thess. 1:5)
In the Believer (Titus 3:5; Gal. 4:6; Rom. 8:15-26)
In the Church (1 Cor. 3:16; 12:4-8; Acts 13:2-4)

36   The Opposition to the Spirit

By the Sinner—Resisted (Acts 7:51; Heb. 10:29)
In the Saint—Grieved (Eph. 4:30, with Isa. 63:10)
In the Church—Quenched (1 Thess. 5:19; 1 Cor. 14:43)

37 Three Foundation Facts

Ruin in Sins (Rom. 5:12; 1 Cor. 15:22; Rom. 3:23; Ps. 51:5;
Eph. 2:1)

Redemption by Blood (Heb. 9:22; Types, Gen. 4:4; Exod.
12:13; Lev. 16:16)

Regeneration by the Spirit (John 3:5; John 6:63; Titus 3:5)

38 Seven Fundamental Truths

The Inspiration of the Scriptures (2 Tim. 3:16)
The Trinity of the Godhead (Matt. 28:19)
The Divinity of the Lord Jesus (John 1:1)
The Atoning Death of Christ (Heb. 9:14)
Justification by Faith alone (Rom. 3:28)
Salvation, Present and Eternal (Heb. 5:9)
Future Punishment of the Wicked (Matt. 25:46)

39 The Inspiration of the Scriptures

Their Divine Origin (2 Tim. 3:16)
The Human Channels (2 Peter 1:21; 2 Sam. 23:2)
Their Absolute Purity (Ps. 19:8; Prov. 30:5)
Their Supreme Authority (Ps. 138:2; 109:128)
Accepted by the Lord Jesus (Luke 24:27-45)
Eternal and Imperishable (Matt. 24:35; 1 Peter 1:25)
Wrested and Corrupted by Men (2 Cor. 2:17; 2 Peter 3:16)
Made Void by Tradition (Mark 7:13; 2 Tim. 4:4)

40 The Eternal Destiny of Man

Two Roads and Two Ends (Matt. 6:13-27)
Two Destinies, Contrasted (1 Peter 4:17-18; Rev. 22:14-15)
Eternal Glory for the Saved (1 Peter 5:10; 2 Tim. 2:10)
Eternal Woe for the Lost (Mark 9:43; 2 Thess. 1:10)

41   The Atonement of Christ

Its Necessity (Heb. 9:22; Job 33:24)
Its Nature (John 1:29; 1 Cor. 15:3; 1 Peter 3:18)
Its Sufficiency (Heb. 9:12, 25-28; 10:10-12; Eph. 5:2)
Its Results (Rom. 3:25-26; Heb. 1:3; 10:17; Col. 1:20)

42   Atonement in Type and Prophecy

Types of Christ (Gen. 3:21; 4:4; 8:20; Num. 21:9)
Types of His Atoning Death (Gen. 6:14; Exod. 12:6; 30:16; Lev. 16:19)
Foreshadowings (Gen. 22:8-10; Exod. 27:1; Lev. 1:3-5)
Prophecies (Isa. 53:4-12; Dan. 9:26; Zech. 13:7)

43   Atonement in Fact and Testimony

Made on the Cross (John 19:30, 34-36; Heb. 9:14)
Accepted in the Heavens (Heb. 9:24; 10:12; 4:14)
Attested by the Resurrection (Acts 13:29-30; Rom. 4:25)
Witnessed to by the Spirit (Heb. 10:15; Acts 5:32)
Proclaimed in the Gospel (1 Cor. 15:3; Acts 10:43; 13:38)
Relied upon by the Believer (Rom. 3:25; 5:1)

44   Atonement in Result and Celebration

It Effects Justification (Rom. 5:8)
It Brings to God (Eph. 2:13)
It Sanctifies (Heb. 10:10; 13:12)
It Cleanses (Rev. 1:5; 1 John 1:7)
It Reconciles (Rom. 5:10; 2 Cor. 5:20-21)
Symbolized in Baptism (Rom. 6:4; Col. 2:12)
Commemorated in the Lord's Supper (1 Cor. 11:23-26)

45   The World: Its Course and End

The Empire of Satan (John 12:31; 16:11; 1 John 5:4)
It has rejected Christ (John 1:10; 7:7)
Christ came to Save (John 3:16-17; 12:47; 1 Tim. 1:15)
All Guilty before God (Rom. 3:19)
Its Judgment (John 12:31; Acts 17:31)
Its Doom (1 John 1:17; 2 Peter 3:6-8)

46   The Christian's Relation
to the World

Born into the World (John 16:21)
Given out of the World (John 17:6)
Delivered from the World (Gal. 1:4)
Crucified to the World (Gal. 6:14)
Not of the World (John 17:16)
A Stranger in the World (1 John 3:2)
Hated by the World (John 17:14)

47 The Christian's Place in the World

Sent into the World (John 17:18, 20:21)
Preaching to the World (Mark 15:15)
The Light of the World (Phil. 2:15; Matt. 5:14)
Live Godly in the World (Titus 2:12)
Not Conformed to the World (Rom. 12:2; John 17:15)
Love not the World (1 John 2:16; 2 Tim. 4:10)
Passing through the World (1 Peter 2:11)
No Friendship with the World (James 4:4; 1:27)

48   Divine Love in Varied Aspects

Love of Compassion (John 3:16)—For Sinners
Love of Relationship (1 John 3:1)—To Children
Love of Communion (John 14:23)—To Obedient Ones

49   Children of God: Their Position
A Title of Relationship and Endearment

Begotten of God (John 1:12; 1 John 5:1-2)
In a New Relationship (Rom. 8:15; John 8:35)
Linked with Christ (John 20:17; Heb. 2:11)
Heirs and Joint Heirs (Gal. 4:7; Rom. 8:17)
Dear Children—Title of Endearment (1 John 2:12-28)
Unknown by the World (1 John 3:2; John 15:18-21)
Waiting for the Manifestation (Rom. 8:19; Col. 3:4)

50   Children of God: Their Progress

New-born Babes—Healthy and Growing (1 Peter 2:1)
Little Children (1 John 2:13-18; 3:18)
Infants, an Unhealthy Condition (Gal. 4:1; 1 Cor. 3:1)
Young Men (1 John 2:14-17; Prov. 20:29)
Fathers, full grown (1 John 2:13-14; 1 Cor. 4:15)

51   Children of God: Their Prospects

They shall see the Lord (1 John 3:2; 1 Cor. 13:12)
They shall be like Him (1 John 3:2; 2 Thess. 1:10)
They will dwell in the Father's House (John 14:2-3)
They will be manifested in glory (Rom. 8:19-21)
They will be forever with the Lord (Rev. 22:7)

52   Sons of God
A Title of Dignity and Manifestation of Character

We become Sons by Faith (Gal. 3:24; John 1:12)
Possess the Spirit of Sons (Gal. 4:6; Rom. 8:14)
To Enjoy the Place of Sons (Luke 15:24; Rom. 8:14)
To Manifest the Character of Sons (Matt. 5:45-48)
Receive the Training of Sons (Heb. 12:5-11; 1 Peter 1:17)
To be Conformed to Christ (Rom. 8:30; 1 John 3:2)

53   The Lordship of Christ

Exalted as Lord (Acts 2:36; Phil. 2:9-10)
All Authority given Him (Matt. 28:18; John 17:2)
Confessed Lord in Conversion (Rom. 10:9)
Sanctified Lord in the Heart (1 Peter 3:15)
Owned as Lord in the Life (Col. 3:17)
Acknowledged Lord in the Church (1 Cor. 14:37)
To be Honored as Lord by all (Phil. 2:10)

BIBLE THEMES

54   Seven "Kingdoms"
In the New Testament

Kingdom of God (John 3:3)
Kingdom of Heaven (Matt. 3:2)
Kingdom of His Dear Son (Col. 1:13)
Kingdom of the Father (Matt. 13:23)
Kingdom of the Son of Man (Luke 1:33)
Kingdom Everlasting (2 Peter 1:11)

55   Seven "Better Things"
In the Epistle to the Hebrews

Better Testament (Heb. 7:22)
Better Sacrifice (Heb. 9:23)
Better Promises (Heb. 8:6)
Better Hope (Heb. 7:19)
Better Substance (Heb. 10:34)
Better Country (Heb. 11:16)
Better Resurrection (Heb. 11:35)

56   Similies of Spiritual Growth

As a Seed (Mark 4:27)—In Steadiness
As a Lily (Hos. 14:5)—In Lowliness
As a Cedar (Ps. 102:12)—In Strength
As a Psalm (Ps. 92:12)—In Uprightness
As a Vine (Hos. 14:7)—In Fruitfulness

57   Threefold Work of the Spirit

The Spirit Regenerating (John 3:5)
The Spirit Indwelling (John 4:14)
The Spirit Outflowing (John 7:38)

58   Christian Readiness

Ready to Answer (1 Peter 3:15)
Ready to Preach (Rom. 1:15)
Ready to Distribute (1 Tim. 4:18)
Ready for every Good Work (Titus 3:1)
Ready to Die (Acts 21:13)
Ready to meet the Lord (Luke 12:36)
Ready to enter the Glory (Matt. 25:10)

59   "Daily" Things in Christian Life

Which maintain the soul in a good condition

Daily Renewing of inner man (2 Cor. 4:16)
Daily Reading of the Word (Neh. 8:18)
Daily Prayer to the Lord (Ps. 76:3)
Daily Praising of the Lord (Ps. 72:15)
Daily Exhortation of one another (Heb. 3:13)
Daily Cross to bear (Luke 9:23)

60   Rest in Seven Aspects

Creation Rest (Gen. 2:2)—Broken by Sin
Redemption Rest (Zeph. 3:17)—Secured in Christ
The Sinner's Rest (Matt. 11:28)—By coming to Christ
The Saint's Rest (Matt. 11:29)—In Learning of Christ
The Servant's Rest (Mark 6:30)—In Communion with Christ
Paradise Rest (Rev. 14:13, with 2 Cor. 5:8)—Present
Eternal Rest (Heb. 4:9; Rev. 22:5)—Future

61   New Creation

A New Birth (John 3:3)—Its Entrance
A New Man (Col. 3:10)—Its Characteristic
A New Life (Rom. 6:4)—Its Manifestation
A New Song (Ps. 40:3)—Its Melody
A New Path (Heb. 10:20)—Its Highway
A New City (Rev. 21:2)—Its Consummation

62   The Life of Faith

Obedience of Faith (Rom. 16:26)—Brings Salvation
Living by Faith (Gal. 2:20)—For Sustenance
Walking by Faith (2 Cor. 5:7)—In Obedience
Praying in Faith (James 5:15)—Brings Blessing
Fighting in Faith (1 Tim. 6:12)—Gives Victory

63   Four Things Belonging to Christ
As seen in the Epistle to the Philippians

The Gospel of Christ (Phil. 1:27)—Our Theme
The Work of Christ (Phil. 2:30)—Our Employment
The Knowledge of Christ (Phil. 3:8)—Our Study
The Power of Christ (Phil. 4:13)—Our Strength

64   The Holy Spirit
In the Believer—Experimentally

Bears Witness (Rom. 8:16)—To Sonship
Sheds Love Abroad (Rom. 5:5)—In Experience
Strengthens (Eph. 3:16)—For Service
Intercedes (Rom. 8:11)—In Prayer
Leads (Rom. 8:14)—In Obedience
Produces Fruit (Gal. 5:22)—In Life
Gives Utterance (Acts 2:4)—In Testimony

65 The Holy Spirit

In the Believer—Officially

In His Heart (Gal. 4:6)—As a Son
On His Person (Eph. 1:13)—As a Seal
In His Body (1 Cor. 6:19)—As a Temple

The *First* establishes communion *with* God
The *Second* secures him *for* God
The *Third* sets him apart *to* God

66 "In the Spirit"

Live in the Spirit (Gal. 5:25)—Christian Life
Walk in the Spirit (Gal. 5:25)—Christian Walk
Pray in the Spirit (Eph. 6:18)—Christian Devotion
Worship in the Spirit (Phil. 3:3)—Christian Priesthood
Love in the Spirit (Col. 1:8)—Christian Brotherhood

67 Christ's Calls to His Own

Arise from Among the Dead (Eph. 5:14)—Separation
Arise, let us go Hence (John 14:31)—Communion
Arise and Walk (Matt. 9:5)—Discipleship
Arise and Come Away (Song of Sol. 2:13)—Glory

68 The Lord's People

Are described in the Word as

A Chosen People (Deut. 7:6; 1 Peter 2:9)
A Redeemed People (Exod. 15:13; Eph. 1:7)
A Peculiar People (Deut. 14:2; Titus 2:14)
A Separated People (Exod. 33:16; John 15:19)
A Holy People (Deut. 7:6; 1 Peter 1:15)
A Happy People (Deut. 33:29; John 15:11)

69 Four "Withouts"

In the Epistle to the Hebrews

"Without Shedding of Blood" (Heb. 9:22)—No Remission
"Without Faith" (Heb. 11:6)—No Pleasing God
"Without Holiness" (Heb. 12:14)—No Heaven
"Without Chastisement" (Heb. 12:8)—No Sonship

70 "Precious" Things in Peter's Epistles

Precious Blood (1 Peter 1:19)—To Redeem
Precious Faith (1 Peter 1:7)—To Try
Precious Stone (1 Peter 2:4)—To Uphold
Precious Christ (1 Peter 2:7)—To Love
Precious Promises (2 Peter 1:4)—To Plead

71 Crowns

Rewards of Faithful Service here

Crown of Life (Rev. 2:16)—The Martyr's Reward
Crown of Righteousness (2 Tim. 4:8)—The Steward's Reward
Crown of Glory (1 Peter 5:4)—The Shepherd's Reward

72 Divine Love in Seven Aspects

Love Manifested (1 John 4:9)—In the Gift of Christ
Love Commended (Rom. 5:8)—At the Cross
Love Bestowed (1 John 3:1)—In our Sonship
Love Believed (1 John 4:16)—By the Sinner
Love Perceived (1 John 3:16)—By the Saint
Love Shed Abroad (Rom. 5:5)—In the Spirit
Love Dwelling (1 John 3:17)—In the Heart

73 The Christian Stewardship

The Master's Appointment (Matt. 25:14; Mark 13:34)
The Steward's Responsibility (1 Cor. 4:1-3; 2 Tim. 2:2)
The Trust Committed (1 Thess. 2:4; 2 Tim. 1:14)
    The Gospel for all (Mark 15:15; Rom. 1:4)
    The Truth, all of it (Matt. 28:20; Acts 20:27)
The Steward's Character (Titus 2:7; 1 Cor. 4:2)
    A Good Steward (1 Peter 4:10)—Dispensing
    A Wise Steward (Luke 12:42)—Discriminating
    An Unjust Steward (Luke 16:1)—Wasting
The Reckoning Day (2 Cor. 5:9; 1 Cor. 4:5)

74 Faith

The Word of Faith (Rom. 10:8)—The Preacher's Message
The Hearing of Faith (Gal. 3:2)—The Hearer's Responsibility
The Obedience of Faith (Rom. 16:16)—The Receiver's Response
The Righteousness of Faith (Rom. 4:13)—The Believer's Position
The Walk of Faith (2 Cor. 5:6)—The Believer's Path
The Work of Faith (1 Thess. 1:3)—The Christian's Service
The Fight of Faith (1 Tim. 6:12)—The Soldier's Warfare

75 Sevenfold View of the Spirit

The Spirit of Life (Rom. 8:2)
The Spirit of Sonship (Rom. 8:15)
The Spirit of Promise (Eph. 1:13)
The Spirit of Power (2 Tim. 1:7)
The Spirit of Truth (John 14:17)
The Spirit of Wisdom (Eph. 1:14)
The Spirit of Glory (1 Peter 4:14)

76   Separation

From the World (John 15:19; Gal. 1:4; 6:14)
From the Darkness (1 Peter 2:9; Eph. 5:8; 2 Cor. 6:14)
From False Professors (2 Tim. 3:1-5; 2 Cor. 6:17)
From Teachers of Error (1 Tim. 1:4; 4:7; 6:5)

77   Amalgamations
Which are Forbidden in God's Word

Of Law and Grace (Acts 15:1-24; Gal. 3:2; 5:4)
Of Truth and Tradition (Mark 6:8-13; 2 Tim. 4:3)
Of Saints and Sinners (2 Cor. 6:14; 2 Tim. 2:21)

78   Seven "New Things"
Which all Believers now Possess

Repentance—A new *Mind* about God (Acts 20:21)
Justification—A new *State* before God (Rom. 4:25)
Regeneration—A new *Life* from God (Titus 3:5)
Conversion—A new *Attitude* toward God (Matt. 18:3)
Sonship—A new *Relationship* with God (1 John 3:1)
Sanctification—A new *Position* before God (Jude 1)
Glorification—A new *Place* with God (Rom. 8:30)

79   Our God
Is Revealed in the Word as

The God of all Grace (1 Peter 5:10)
The God of Peace (Heb. 13:20)
The God of all Comfort (2 Cor. 1:3)
The God of Patience (Rom. 15:5)
The God of Hope (Rom. 15:13)
The God of Glory (Acts 7:2)
    "Thus God is OUR God for ever" (Ps. 48:14)

80 Living

The Living God (1 Tim. 4:10)—Our Trust
The Living Christ (1 Peter 2:4)—Our Foundation
The Living Spirit (John 4:11)—Our Refreshment
The Living Way (Heb. 10:20)—Our Access
The Living Hope (1 Peter 1:3)—Our Expectation

81 In the Name

Salvation in the Name (Acts 4:12)
Remission in the Name (Acts 10:43)
Baptized in the Name (Acts 19:5)
Gathered unto the Name (Matt. 18:20)
Going Forth in the Name (3 John 7)
Suffering for the Name (1 Peter 4:16)
Not denying the Name (Rev. 3:8)

82 Progress in Grace

Saved by Grace (Eph. 2:9)
Standing in Grace (Rom. 5:2)
Taught by Grace (Titus 2:12)
Growing in Grace (2 Peter 3:18)
Speaking in Grace (Col. 4:6)
Ministering Grace (1 Peter 4:10)

83 Partakers

Of His Promise in Christ (Eph. 3:6)—Salvation
Of the Divine Nature (2 Peter 2:4)—Regeneration
Of the Inheritance (Col. 1:12)—Competency
Of the Heavenly Calling (Heb. 3:1)—Position
Of Christ's Sufferings (1 Peter 4:13)—Discipleship
Of Fatherly Chastisement (Heb. 12:6)—Discipline
Of the Glory (1 Peter 5:1)—Prospect

84 Seven Jehovah Titles

Jehovah-jireh—The Lord will Provide (Gen. 22:14)
Jehovah-tsidkenu—The Lord our Righteousness (Jer. 23:6)
Jehovah-ropheka—The Lord our Healer (Exod. 15:26)
Jehovah-shalom—The Lord our Peace (Judg. 6:24)
Jehovah-rophi—The Lord our Shepherd (Ps. 23:1)
Jehovah-nissi—The Lord our Banner (Exod. 17:15)
Jehovah-shammah—The Lord is there (Ezek. 48:35)

These seven *titles* embrace all the fulness of Jehovah's Name manifested in Christ for His people, completely meeting all their need from guilt to glory.

85 Godliness

The Form of Godliness (2 Tim. 3:5)—The Hypocrite
The Mystery of Godliness (1 Tim. 3:16)—The Savior
The Doctrine of Godliness (1 Tim. 6:3)—The Truth
The Profession of Godliness (1 Tim. 2:15)—The Believer's Confession
The Practice of Godliness (1 Tim. 4:7)—The Believer's Walk
The Pursuit of Godliness (1 Tim. 6:11)—The Believer's Object

86 The Believer's Heart

A Broken Heart (Ps. 51:17)—Confesses Sin
An Opened Heart (Acts 16:14)—Receives the Word
A Single Heart (Eph. 6:5)—Serves Faithfully
A Pure Heart (1 Peter 1:22)—Loves Fervently
A True Heart (Heb. 10:22)—Draws Near to God
A Purposed Heart (Acts 11:23)—Cleaves to the Lord
An Evil Heart (Heb. 3:12)—Departs from God

87   Divine Unity

Children in one Family—One Father (John 20:17)
Disciples in one School—One Teacher (John 13:13-35)
Sheep in one Flock—One Shepherd (John 10:16)
Members of one Body—One Head (Eph. 4:15)
Stones in one Building—One Foundation (1 Cor. 3:11)

88   Salvation Sevenfold

Saved by Grace (Eph. 2:5)—Actually
Saved through Faith (Eph. 2:8)—Instrumentally
Saved by Works (James 2:14)—Evidentially
Saved through Water (1 Peter 3:21)—Confessedly
Saved by His Life (Rom. 5:9)—Practically
Saved in Hope (Rom. 8:24)—Prospectively
Saved at His Coming (Phil. 3:20)—Eternally

89   Sevenfold Virtue of Christ's Blood

It procures Redemption (Eph. 1:6)
It secures Justification (Rom. 5:9)
It ensures Cleansing (1 John 1:7)
It makes Peace (Col. 1:20)
It effects Sanctification (Heb. 13:12)
It gives Nearness (Eph. 2:13)
It brings Victory (Rev. 12:11)

90   The Word of God

Its Divine Inspiration (2 Tim. 3:16)
Its Absolute Purity (Ps. 12:6)
Its Supreme Authority (Ps. 119:128)
Its Perfect Unity (John 10:35)
Its Eternal Permanency (1 Peter 1:25)
    Other texts on each branch of the subject abound

91   Divine Discipline

Its Subjects: Believers (Heb. 12:5-7; 2 Sam. 7:14; Amos 3:3)
Its Nature: Parental, not judicial (1 Peter 1:14-17; 1 Cor. 11:32)
Its Instruments: The Word (Titus 2:12); The Knife (John 15:4, etc.)
Its Objects: Profit, Fruit, Holiness (Heb. 12:10-11)

92   Divine Riches

Riches of Mercy (Eph. 2:4)
Riches of Grace (Eph. 1:7)
Riches of Goodness (Rom. 2:4)
Riches of Glory (Phil. 4:19)

93   The Lamb of God

The Lamb Provided (Gen. 22:8; Job 33:24)
The Lamb Described (Exod. 12:5-6; 1 Peter 1:19)
The Lamb Revealed (John 1:29-36; Matt. 11:29)
The Lamb Slain (Exod. 12:6-7; Isa. 53:7)
The Lamb Glorified (Rev. 5:6-12; 7:17)
The Lamb Reigning (Rev. 22:1-3)

94   Divine Revelations

The word "Revelation" means Unveiling

God's righteousness revealed (Rom. 1:17)—In the Gospel
Christ revealed (Gal. 1:16)—To the Soul
The Mystery revealed (Eph. 2:3)—Union with Christ
The Glory to be revealed (Rom. 8:18)—At His Coming
The Man of Sin revealed (2 Thess. 2:8)—To Christ Rejecters

95   Eternal Blessings

Purchased with an Eternal Redemption (Heb. 9:12)
Saved with an Eternal Salvation (Heb. 5:9)
Possessed of an Eternal Life (John 3:15)
Called to an Eternal Glory (1 Peter 5:10)
Waiting for an Eternal Home (2 Cor. 5:1)

96   "At Jesus' Feet"

For Forgiveness (Luke 7:38)
For Healing (Matt. 15:3)
For Teaching (Luke 10:39)
In Distress (John 11:32)
In Prayer (Luke 8:41)
In Fear (Rev. 1:17)
In Worship (Luke 17:16)

97   Christ, Our Keeper

Kept by His Power (1 Peter 1:5)
Kept from falling (Jude 24)
Kept from all evil (2 Thess. 3:3)
Kept in Peace (Isa. 26:3)
Kept as the Apple of His Eye (Deut. 32:10)
Kept from the temptation (Rev. 3:10)
Kept for eternal glory (John 17:12)

98   Suffering for Christ

Suffering for Righteousness' sake (1 Peter 3:14)
Suffering for godly living (2 Tim. 2:12)
Suffering for the Kingdom of God (2 Thess. 1:5)
Suffering as a Christian (1 Peter 4:16)
Suffering for Christ's sake (Phil. 1:29)
Suffering and Glory (1 Peter 5:1)

99   Jesus Christ, Our Lord

Exalted as Lord (Acts 2:36)
Confessed as Lord (Rom. 10:9)
Owned as Lord (Acts 9:6)
Praised as Lord (Ps. 9:11)
Obeyed as Lord (Col. 3:17)
Served as Lord (Col. 3:24)
Denied as Lord (Jude 14)

100   The Christian Pilgrim

(1 Peter 2:11, with Hebrews 11:13)

His Path (Heb. 13:13)
His Support (Phil. 4:13)
His Foes (1 Peter 2:11)
His Temptations (James 1:2)
His City Home (Heb. 11:10)
His Friends (Heb. 11:13)
His Inheritance (1 Peter 1:4)

101   New Testament Mysteries

The Mystery of Godliness (1 Tim. 3:16)—Christ Personally
The Mystery Kept Secret (Rom. 16:25)—The Truth Revealed
The Mystery of the Faith (1 Tim. 3:9)—The Truth Held Fast
The Mystery of Christ (Eph. 5:31-32)—Christ and the Church
The Mystery of Union (Eph. 3:3)—Jew and Gentile One
The Mystery of Lawlessness (2 Thess. 2:7)—Satan's Counterfeits
The Mystery of Glorification (1 Cor. 15:31)—At Christ's Coming

102 The People of God

Are

A Saved People (Deut. 33:29)
A Separated People (Lev. 20:24)
A Happy People (Ps. 144:15)
A Holy People (Deut. 7:6)
A Peculiar People (1 Peter 2:9)

103 What the Gospel Brings

To all who Believe it

Saved by the Gospel (Rom. 1:16)
Begotten through the Gospel (1 Cor. 4:15)
Peace received in the Gospel (Rom. 10:15)
Blessing through the Gospel (Rom. 15:29)
Glory revealed by the Gospel (1 Tim. 1:11)

104 Things That Accompany Salvation

(Hebrews 6:9)

The *Knowledge* of Salvation (Luke 1:77)
The *Joy* of Salvation (Ps. 51:12)
The *Strength* of Salvation (Isa. 33:6)
The *Wells* of Salvation (Isa. 12:3)
The *Cup* of Salvation (Ps. 116:13)
The *Hope* of Salvation (Eph. 6:17)

105 "With Christ"

Dead with Christ (Rom. 6:4)
Buried with Christ (Col. 2:12)
Quickened with Christ (Col. 2:12)
Risen with Christ (Col. 3:1)
Glorified with Christ (Rom. 8:17)

106 The Christian Path

Walk in Light (1 John 1:7)
Walk in Love (Eph. 5:2)
Walk in the Spirit (Gal. 5:16)
Walk in Truth (3 John 4)
Walk in Good Works (Eph. 2:10)
Walk in Wisdom (Col. 4:5)
Walk Circumspectly (Eph. 5:15)

107 A Seven-linked Chain of Fellowship

Fellow-heirs (Eph. 3:6)—Of One Inheritance
Fellow-members (Eph. 3:6)—Of One Body
Fellow-partakers (Eph. 3:6)—Of One Calling
Fellow-citizens (Eph. 2:19)—Of One Home
Fellow-laborers (Phil. 4:3)—Of One Master
Fellow-soldiers (Phil. 2:25)—In One Warfare
Fellow-prisoners (Rom. 16:7)—With One Hope

108 The Unequal Yoke

Forbidden Between Saved and Unsaved

In Matrimony (1 Cor. 7:39, with Deut. 7:3)
In Commerce (Deut. 22:10; Amos 3:2)
In Religion (2 Cor. 6:14; 2 Tim. 3:5)
In Social Circle (Eph. 5:7-11; Rom. 12:2)

The *First* was ignored by Israel (Judg. 2:6; Neh. 13:23)
The *Second* set aside by Dinah (Gen. 34:1)
The *Third* disobeyed by Jehoshaphat (2 Chron. 20:35)
The *Fourth* transgressed by the Young Prophet (1 Kings 13:17-22)

109 God's Truth in Divine Order

Key Words of the First Seven Books

In *Genesis* is the *Election* and *Call* of God's People
In *Exodus*, their *Redemption* and *Separation*
In *Leviticus*, their *Acceptance* and *Worship*
In *Numbers*, their *Walk* and *Warfare*
In *Deuteronomy*, their *Government* and *Testimony*
In *Joshua*, their *Warfare* and *Inheritance*
In *Judges*, their *Declension* and *Defeat*

110 Divine Fulness

Fulness of Grace (John 1:16)—Our Resource
Fulness of Blessing (Rom. 15:29)—Our Privilege
Fulness of Joy (John 15:11)—Our Portion
Fulness of Power (Acts 6:8)—Our Strength
Fulness of God (Eph. 3:19)—Our Consummation

111 Sins Against the Holy Spirit

He is Resisted (Acts 7:51)—By the World
He is Grieved (Eph. 4:30)—By the Believer
He is Quenched (1 Thess. 5:19)—In the Church

The *First* is by Rejection of the Gospel
The *Second* through trifling with Sin
The *Third* by man's arrangements hindering His work

112 Holiness

Its Pattern in Christ (Acts 4:27)
Its Standard in the Word (2 Peter 2:21; Col. 1:22)
How Produced (Eph. 1:4; 4:24; 5:27)
How Maintained (1 Tim. 4:12; 2 Tim. 2:21)
Personal (1 Peter 1:15; 2 Peter 3:11)
Social (2 Cor. 7:1; 1 Thess. 4:7)
Ecclesiastical (Ps. 93:5; 1 Cor. 3:11)

113   Vital Godliness

The Word means Piety, Reverence

Its Lack in the World (Ps. 12:1)
Its Empty Form in Christendom (2 Tim. 3:5)
Its Pattern and Source in Christ (1 Tim. 3:16; Heb. 5:7)
Its Power for Believers (2 Peter 1:3; 2 Tim. 3:16)
Its Pursuit by Believers (1 Tim. 4:7; 6:11)
Its Treatment from the World (2 Tim. 3:12)
Its Importance in View of Eternity (2 Peter 3:16)

114   Secret of a Peaceful Life

Peace with God (Rom. 5:1)—By Faith
Peace Multiplied (2 Peter 1:2)—Through Knowledge
Peace of God (Phil. 4:6-7)—By Prayerfulness
Peace Ruling (Col. 3:15)—In Submission
God of Peace (Phil. 4:9)—By Obedience
Great Peace (Ps. 119:165)—By Loving the Word
Perfect Peace (Isa. 26:3)—Through Trusting

115   Temptation

Trials, tests: sent or allowed by God

Divers Temptations (James 1:2)—Of various kinds
Manifold Temptations (1 Peter 1:6)—From various sources
Their Origin, Flesh (James 1:14); Devil (1 Thess. 3:5)
Their Uses, Test (1 Peter 1:7); Strengthen (1 Peter 5:10)
The Way of Victory (James 1:12)—Endurance
The Power of Deliverance (1 Cor. 10:12; 2 Peter 2:8-9)
The Result and Reward (James 1:2-12)

BIBLE SUBJECTS

116   Four Titles of Believers
In John 15
Disciples (v. 8)—Learning of Christ
Friends (v. 15)—Communing with Christ
Servants (v. 20)—Working for Christ
Witnesses (v. 27)—Testifying to Christ

117   Three Circles for Prayer
"All Saints" (Eph. 6:18, with Col. 1:3; 4:12)
"All Men" (1 Tim. 2:1, with Matt. 5:14)
"All Things" (Matt. 21:12, with Phil. 4:6)

118   A Threefold Manner of Life
"Soberly"—in regard to ourselves (Rom. 12:3)
"Righteously"—in respect of the world (Prov. 2:20)
"Godly"—in relation to God (2 Tim. 3:12)

119   The Calling of the Believers
Called out of Darkness (1 Peter 2:9)
Called Saints (Rom. 1:7)
Called Sons of God (1 John 3:1)
Called by Grace (Gal. 1:15)
Called to Glory (1 Peter 5:9)
Called unto Fellowship (1 Cor. 1:9)
Called into Liberty (Gal. 5:13)
   "Walk worthy of the calling" (Eph. 4:1)

120   Four Aspects of Christian Life

Sons to love (1 John 5:2; Col. 1:4)
Servants to obey (2 Tim. 2:24; Rom. 6:22)
Soldiers to fight (2 Tim. 2:3; 1 Tim. 6:12)
Stewards to occupy (Titus 1:7; Luke 19:13)

121   Three Attitudes of the Servant of the Lord

Sitting before the Lord (2 Sam. 7:18)—In Rest
Standing before the Lord (1 Kings 17:1)—In Readiness
Speaking before the Lord (2 Cor. 12:19)—In Testimony

122   The Christian's Conversation

His *former* Conversation (Eph. 4:22)
Was "Vain" (1 Peter 1:18)
Or "Filthy" (2 Peter 2:7)

It is now
"Holy" before God (1 Peter 3:11)
"Chaste" in the Home (1 Peter 3:1)
"Honest" in the Business (1 Peter 2:12)
"Good" in the World (1 Peter 3:16)

123   Symbols of God's Care

Of His People
As a *Mother* comforteth (Isa. 66:13)
As a *Father* pitieth (Ps. 103:13)
As a *Nurse* cherisheth (1 Thess. 2:7)
As a *Shepherd* seeketh (Ezek. 34:12)
As a *Hen* gathereth (Matt. 23:37)
As an *Eagle* fluttereth (Deut. 32:11)
As a *Bridegroom* rejoiceth (Isa. 62:5)

124   A Sevenfold Use of the Word

Born Again by the Word (1 Peter 1:23; James 1:18)
Cleansed by the Word (Eph. 5:26; Ps. 119:9)
Saved by the Word (1 Tim. 4:16; James 1:21)
Growing by the Word (1 Peter 2:2; Jer. 15:16)
Sanctified by the Word (John 17:17; 1 Tim. 4:5)
Enlightened by the Word (Ps. 19:8; 119:105)
Kept by the Word (Ps. 17:4; Rev. 3:10)

125   The Believer's Heavenly Possessions

A *Savior* in Heaven (Acts 5:31; Phil. 3:20)
A *Master* in Heaven (Eph. 6:9; Acts 9:6)
His *Name* written in Heaven (Luke 10:20; Phil. 4:3)
His *Citizenship* in Heaven (Phil. 3:20; Heb. 12:22)
His *Hope* in Heaven (Col. 1:5; 1 John 3:3)
His *Inheritance* in Heaven (1 Peter 1:4; Eph. 1:3)
His *Reward* in Heaven (Luke 6:23; Rev. 22:12)

126   God's Infinite Things

Riches that are unsearchable (Eph. 3:8)
Joy that is unspeakable (1 Peter 1:8)
Peace that passeth understanding (Phil. 4:7)
Love that passeth knowledge (Eph. 3:19)
Ways past finding out (Rom. 11:33)

127   Things in Which to "Abound"

Abound in Faith (2 Cor. 8:7)
Abound in Hope (Rom. 15:13)
Abound in Love (Phil. 1:9)
Abound in Good Works (2 Cor. 9:8)

128   Things "Laid Up" for Believers

The Lord's Goodness (Ps. 31:19)
The Hope of Glory (Col. 1:5)
The Crown of Righteousness (2 Tim. 4:6)

129   "Consider Him"

In Humiliation (Heb. 12:3)—Our Example
In Exaltation (Heb. 3:1)—Our Representative

130   The Powers of Satan

Satan's Seat (Rev. 2:13)—His Political Power (John 12:31)
Satan's Depths (Rev. 2:24)—His Deceptive Wiles (Rev. 20:3-10)
Satan's Synagogue (Rev. 3:9)—His Religious Devices (2 Cor. 4:4)
In the *First* he appears as "a Roaring Lion" (1 Peter 5:9)
In the *Second* as a Subtle Serpent (2 Cor. 10:3)
In the *Third* as an Angel of Light (2 Cor. 10:14)

131   "Unto Him"

"Unto Him shall the gathering of the people be"
(Genesis 49:10)

For Salvation (Luke 15:1)
For Teaching (Mark 6:30)
For Worship (Heb. 13:3)
For Fellowship (Matt. 18:20)
In Glory (2 Thess. 2:1)

132   Abundant Grace

Grace to Save (Eph. 2:9)
Grace to Establish (Heb. 13:9)
Grace to Sustain (2 Cor. 9:8)
Grace to Serve (1 Cor. 15:10)

133   The Name of Jesus

The Source of *Salvation* (Acts 4:12)
The Authority in *Baptism* (Acts 10:48)
The Center of *Gathering* (Matt. 18:20)
The Power in *Discipline* (1 Cor. 5:4)
The Motive in *Service* (3 John 7)
The Plea in *Prayer* (John 14:14)
The Rule in *Everything* (Col. 3:17)

134   "All Saints"

In the Epistle to the Ephesians

"Love *to* all Saints" (Eph. 1:15)
"Comprehend *with* all Saints" (Eph. 3:18)
"Prayer *for* all Saints" (Eph. 6:18)

135   Fellowship in Four Aspects

Fellowship of Life (1 John 1:1-3)
Fellowship in Light (1 John 1:7)
Fellowship of the Church (1 Cor. 1:10; Acts 2:42)
Fellowship in Service (1 Cor. 3:9; Col. 4:10)

136   Christ in Hebrews

The Sinpurger (Heb. 1:3)—To Clear
The Victor (Heb. 2:15)—To Deliver
The Apostle (Heb. 3:1)—To Speak
The High Priest (Heb. 4:14)—To Succor
The Forerunner (Heb. 7:20)—To Represent
The Coming One (Heb. 10:37)—To Welcome

137   Threefold Rejoicing

In God's Salvation (Ps. 60:14, with 1 Peter 1:6)
In Christ Jesus (Phil. 3:3, with 1 Peter 1:8)
In the Lord (Phil. 4:10, with Hab. 3:18)

138   A Double Testimony for Christ

By a Young Convert

Go home and *tell* (Mark 5:19)—The Lips
Return and *show* (Luke 8:39)—The Life

139   A Good Minister

As seen in Apollos (Acts 18:24-25)

"An Eloquent Man"
"Mighty in the Scriptures"
"Instructed in the way of the Lord"
"Fervent in Spirit"

These four when combined, make "a good minister of Jesus Christ" (1 Tim. 4:6).

140   "Till He Come"

Show the Lord's Death (1 Cor. 11:26)—Worshipers
Hold Fast His Truth (Rev. 2:25)—Warriors
Occupy in His Service (Luke 19:13)—Workers

141   Our Calling

Called Sons of God (1 John 3:1)—By the Father
Called Christians (Acts 11:26)—By the Son
Called Saints (Rom. 1:7)—By the Spirit

142   Three Great Gospel Blessings

Procured at the Cross, Proclaimed in the Gospel

Remission of Sins (Acts 10:43; Heb. 10:18)
Reconciliation to God (2 Cor. 5:20; Rom. 5:10)
Regeneration by the Spirit (Titus 3:5; 1 Peter 1:23)

143   Two Conditions of Heart

A *True* Heart (Heb. 10:22)—Draws near to God
An *Evil* Heart (Heb. 3:12)—Departs from God

144   Prayer

The place for Prayer, "Everywhere" (1 Tim. 2:8)
The time for Prayer, "Always" (Luke 18:1)
Subjects for Prayer, "Everything" (Phil. 4:6)
Answers to Prayer, "All Things" (Matt. 21:12)
Conditions of Prayer, "In My Name" (John 14:14)

145   Seven "I Wills" of the Believer
A Full Confession of Faith

"I will trust and not be afraid" (Isa. 12:2)
"I will bless the Lord" (Ps. 34:11)
"I will love Thee, O Lord" (Ps. 18:1)
"I will keep Thy statutes" (Ps. 119:145)
"I will walk before the Lord" (Ps. 118:9)
"I will praise Thee" (Ps. 139:14)
"I will behave myself wisely" (Ps. 101:2)

146   Christ's Present Work
for His People

He saves them (Rom. 5:10)
He appears for them (Heb. 9:24)
He makes intercession (Rom. 8:34)
He keeps them (Jude 24)
He cleanses them (Eph. 5:26)
He restores them (Ps. 23:2)
He leads them (John 10:4)

147   Jesus Christ, Our Object

Looking unto Jesus (Heb. 12:2)—Our Example
Learning of Jesus (Luke 10:39)—Our Teacher
Leaning on Jesus (Song of Sol. 8:5)—Our Strength
Looking for Jesus (Phil. 3:20)—Our Hope

148   A Disciple of Christ

His Credentials and Character

His Master (John 13:14)
His Book (2 Tim. 3:16)
His Clothing (1 Peter 5:5)
His Badge (John 13:35)
His Cross (Luke 14:27)
His Companions (Ps. 119:63)
His Fruit (John 15:8)

149   Saints of New Testament Time

Showing Varied Spiritual Conditions

Believing *Romans* (Rom. 1:8)
Progressive *Thessalonians (2 Thess. 1:3)*
Obedient *Philippians* (Phil. 2:12)
Loving *Colossians* (Col. 1:4)
Faithful *Ephesians* (Eph. 1:1)
Carnal *Corinthians* (1 Cor. 3:3)
Foolish *Galatians* (Gal. 3:1)

150   Union With Christ and One Another

In Four Aspects

Members of the Body (Eph. 4:15-16)—Christ the Head
Branches in the Vine (John 15:5)—Christ the Stem
Stones in the Building (Eph. 2:20-22)—Christ the Corner
Sheep of a Flock (Acts 20:28)—Christ the Shepherd

151   Christ's Gifts to His People

He gave His Life (John 10:1-5)
He gave Himself (Gal. 2:20)
He gives His Spirit (1 John 3:24)
He gave His Words (John 17:8)
He gives His Peace (John 14:27)
He gave His Example (John 13:15)
He gives His Glory (John 17:22)

152   Three Great Changes

In which all Believers Share

Translated at Conversion (Col. 1:13; Acts 26:18)
Transformed by Contemplation (2 Cor. 3:18; Rom. 12:2)
Transfigured at Glorification (Phil. 3:1; John 3:2)

153   Five Relations of Believers

Children in Relationship (1 John 1:12)
Sons in Dignity (Rom. 8:14)
Priests in Nearness (1 Peter 2:5)
Saints in Separateness (Eph. 5:3)
Kings in Authority (Rev. 1:6)

154   Christ, the Living One

A Living Stone (1 Peter 2:4)—To Rest Upon
A Living Way (Heb. 10:26)—To Draw Near Through
A Living Priest (Heb. 7:25)—To Represent Us
A Living Hope (1 Peter 1:3)—To Wait For

155   Obedience to God

The Proof of Conversion (Rom. 6:16)
The Recognition of God (Acts 5:29)
The Mark of Children (1 Peter 1:14)
The Manifestation of Love (John 14:15)

156   Four Rests

Rest to the Conscience (Matt. 11:28)—In Christ
Rest for the Heart (Matt. 11:29)—Under Christ
Rest amid Service (Mark 6:30)—With Christ
Rest in Heaven (Heb. 4:9)—Like Christ

157   Saved

By God (2 Tim. 1:9)—The Source
Through Grace (Eph. 2:5)—The Spring
In Christ (John 10:9)—The Cause
By Faith (Luke 7:50)—The Means
By Christ Risen (Rom. 5:10)—The Security
In Hope (Rom. 8:24)—The Consummation

158   Groaning

The Sinner's Groan (Exod. 2:24)—For Deliverance
The Savior's Groan (John 11:33)—In Sympathy
The Spirit's Groan (Rom. 8:26)—Of Witnessing
The Saint's Groan (2 Cor. 5:2-4)—For Emancipation
Creation's Groan (Rom. 8:22)—For Glory

159   The Saint's Sacrifices

His Praise (Heb. 13:15)
His Body (Rom. 12:1)
His Service (Phil. 2:17)
His Means (Phil. 4:18)

160 The Authority of the Lord Jesus
The word "Power" is "Authority"

Over all Flesh (John 17:2)
In Heaven and on Earth (Matt. 28:18)
To Forgive Sins (Matt. 11:6)
To Execute Judgment (John 5:27)

161 Revival in Three Stages

"Revive Me" (Ps. 138:7)
"Revive Us" (Ps. 85:6)
"Revive Thy Work" (Hab. 3:2)

This is God's order, and must not be reversed.

162 Three Lines of Truth

Christ Truth, John's Subject (See John 1:1-3)
Church Truth, Paul's Theme (See Eph. 3:5-7)
Kingdom Truth, Peter, James, and Jude (1 Peter 2:9)

163 A Triplet in Philippians 4

Careful for Nothing (v. 6)—No Burdens
Prayerful for Everything (v. 6)—No Reserves
Thankful for Anything (v. 6)—No Murmurs

164 Christ, the Beloved

Accepted in the Beloved (Eph. 1:6)—Our Place
Listening to the Beloved (Song 2:8)—Our Attitude
Leaning on the Beloved (Song 8:5)—Our Dependence
Speaking of the Beloved (Song 5:10-16)—Our Testimony
Waiting for the Beloved (Song 8:14)—Our Hope

165 Three Aspects of the Spirit's Work
(John 16)

To Glorify God (John 16:14)
To Convict Sinners (John 16:8)
To Instruct Saints (John 16:14)

166. Christ, the Shepherd

The Good Shepherd (John 10:1)—Dying
The Great Shepherd (Hab. 13:20)—Living
The Chief Shepherd (1 Peter 5:4)—Coming

167   Exhortation

Let the peace of God rule in your hearts (Col. 3:15)—Peace
Let the Word of Christ dwell in you (Col. 3:16)—Strength
Let His mind be in you (Phil. 2:5)—Conformity
Let your moderation be known unto all (Phil. 4:5)—
    Character
Let your conversation be without covetousness (Heb. 13:5)
    —Conduct
Let your light so shine before men (Matt. 5:16)—Testimony
Let your loins be girded about (Luke 12:36)—Watchfulness

168   Three Walks

Before God (Gen. 17:1)—Reality
After God (Deut. 13:4)—Obedience
With God (Gen. 5:22)—Communion

169   Seven Aspects of Christian Life

(1 Peter 2)

Babes (1 Peter 2:2)—Feeding
Living Stones (1 Peter 2:5)—Builded
A Holy Priesthood (1 Peter 2:5)—Worshiping
Strangers (1 Peter 2:11)—Away from Home
Pilgrims (1 Peter 2:11)—Going Home
Servants (1 Peter 2:18)—Obeying
Sufferers (1 Peter 2:20)—Submitting

170   In the Heart

The Love of God shed abroad (Rom. 5:5)
The Peace of God ruling (Col. 3:15)
Christ Himself indwelling (Eph. 3:17)

171   The Believer's Feet

Set on a Rock (Ps. 40:2)—Salvation
Cleansed by the Word (John 13:10)—Communion
Kept by Divine Power (1 Sam. 2:9)—Preservation
Shod with Peace (Eph. 6:15)—Warfare
Running with the Gospel (Rom. 10:15)—Service
Bruising Satan (Rom. 16:20)—Victory

172   Love in Four Aspects

The Son's Love to the Father (John 14:3)
The Father's Love to the Son (John 15:9)
The Son's Love to the Saint (John 15:9)
The Saint's Love to one another (John 15:12)

173   Three Offices of the Lord Jesus

Savior (Luke 2:11)—Past
Priest (Heb. 4:14)—Present
Bridegroom (Matt. 25:6)—Future

174   "Stand Fast"

Stand fast in the *Liberty* (Gal. 5:1)—Decision
Stand fast in the *Faith* (1 Cor. 16:11)—Devotion
Stand fast in the *Lord* (Phil. 4:1)—Discipleship
Stand fast in one *Spirit* (Phil. 1:27)—Unity

175   Christ's Three Gifts

To all His Redeemed People

Eternal Life (John 17:4)
The Word (John 17:14)
The Glory (John 17:22)

176 The Spirit's Threefold Witness

"He shall bear witness of Me" (John 15:26)—Revelation
"Ye shall be witnesses *unto* Me" (Acts 1:8)—Declaration
"Our Gospel came in the Holy Spirit" (1 Thess. 1:5)—
  Attestation
The *First* is the Spirit's witness *to* us of Christ
The *Second*, the Spirit's witness *through* us for Christ
The *Third*, the Spirit's witness *in* others to Christ

177 Satan and the World

The "Prince" of this world (John 12:31)—Politically
The "God" of this world (2 Cor. 4:4)—Religiously

178 Walking Worthy

Walk worthy of God (1 Thess. 2:12)
Walk worthy of the Lord (Col. 1:10)
Walk worthy of the Vocation (Eph. 4:1)

179 Two Periods

Fulness of Time (Gal. 4:4)—The Incarnation
Fulness of the Times (Eph. 1:10)—The Millennium
  The former is connected with Christ's Humiliation, the
latter with Christ's manifested Glory.

180 Salvation in Three Aspects

Saved by Christ's Death (Rom. 5:9)—From Sin's Penalty
Saved by Christ's Life (Rom. 5:10)—From Sin's Power
Saved at Christ's Coming (Rom. 13:11)—From Sin's
  Presence

181 Three Christ-filled Psalms

Psalm 22, The Cross—A Suffering Christ
Psalm 23, The Crook—A Risen Christ
Psalm 24, The Crown—A Reigning Christ

182   Three Looks

Backward Look (Isa. 45:22)—To The Dying One
Upward Look (Heb. 12:2)—To the Living One
Onward Look (Titus 2:13)—To The Coming One

183   The Word of God

Regenerating (1 Peter 1:23)
Feeding (1 Peter 2:2)
Sanctifying (John 17:17)
Upbuilding (Acts 20:32)
Enlightening (Ps. 119:105)

184   Faith in Varied Stages

No Faith (Matt. 16:8)—The Unbeliever
Little Faith (Matt. 15:28)—The Doubter
Growing Faith (2 Thess. 1:3)—The Healthy Saint
Strong Faith (Rom. 4:20)—The Aged Pilgrim
Full of Faith (Acts 6:8)—The Fearless Saint

185 The Believer's Standing and State

Saved by Christ (2 Tim. 1:9)—His Place
Sanctified in Christ (1 Cor. 1:2)—His Position
Separated to Christ (Ps. 4:3)—His Path
Satisfied with Christ (Ps. 63:5)—His Portion
Swift for Christ (Ps. 147:15)—His Practice

186   Joy

In Three Stages of Christian Life

At its Beginning (Acts 8:8-39; 16:34; 1 Thess. 1:6)
Throughout its Course (1 Peter 1:8; 1 John 1:4)
At its Close (Acts 20:24; 2 Tim. 4:7)

187   The Christian Conflict

Internal, with the Flesh (Gal. 5:17); not after the flesh (2 Cor. 10:3); with the Armor of light (Rom. 13:12)

External, with the World (John 16:33); not by resistance but submission; with the Armor of righteousness (2 Cor. 6:7)

Infernal, with the Devil (Eph. 6:12); not by submission but resistance (James 4:7); with the whole Armor of God (Eph. 6:13)

188 The Believer's Places of Privilege

In Relation to the Lord Jesus

In His Hand (John 10:28)—Place of Security
On His Shoulder (Luke 15:5)—Place of Strength
In His Bosom (John 13:25)—Place of Learning
At His Feet (Luke 10:39)—Place of Communion

189   A Threefold Choice

Of all Believers in Christ

Chosen to Salvation and Glory (2 Thess. 2:13)
Chosen for Heavenly Position and Holiness (Eph. 1:4)
Chosen unto Separation and Service (1 Peter 1:2)

190   The Shadow of His Wings

Place of Refuge (Ps. 57:1)
Place of Security (Ps. 36:7)
Place of Rejoicing (Ps. 63:7)

191   Two Seekers

Christ seeking Sinners (Luke 19:10)
The Father seeking Worshipers (John 4:23)

192   Key Words to the Four Gospels

Matthew—"Behold Your King" (John 19:14)
Mark—"Behold My Servant" (Isa. 42:1)
Luke—"Behold The Man" (John 19:5)
John—"Behold Your God" (Isa. 40:9)

193   The Service of Christ

Past—"He came to minister" (Mark 10:45)
Present—"He is a minister of the sanctuary" (Heb. 8:2)
Future—"He shall come forth and serve" (Luke 12:37)

194   Sorrow and Joy

Christ's Exceeding Sorrow (Mark 14:34)—In View of the
    Cross
Christ's Exceeding Joy (Jude 24)—In Presence of His Glory

195   The Blessed Man

As Portrayed in the Psalms

The Forgiven Man (Ps. 33:1)
The Trusting Man (Ps. 34:8)
The Separated Man (Ps. 1:1)
The Disciplined Man (Ps. 94:12)
The Obedient Man (Ps. 112:1)

196   Three Conditions of Soul

(Psalms 63)

"My soul thirsteth" (Ps. 63:8)—Desire
"My soul shall be satisfied" (Ps. 63:15)—Decision
"My soul followeth hard" (Ps. 63:24)—Devotion

197   Three Aspects of Faith

Looking *to* Christ (Isa. 45:22)—For Salvation
Leaning *on* Christ (John 13:23)—In Communion
Living *unto* Christ (2 Cor. 5:15)—In Service

198   Continuing

In the Love of Christ (John 15:9)
In the Word of Christ (John 8:31)
In the Grace of God (Acts 13:43)
In the Faith (Acts 14:22)
In the Things Learned (2 Tim. 3:14)

199   Jesus Christ, the Lord

Jesus—The Savior (Matt. 1:21)—For Me
Christ—The Anointed (Gal. 2:20)—In Me
Lord—The Owner (John 13:11)—Over Me

200   Walking Worthy

Of God (1 Thess. 2:12)—Whose Children we are
Of the Lord (Col. 1:10)—Whose Servants we are
Of our Vocation (Eph. 4:1)—Whose Exponents we are

201   The Joy of Angels

In Creation's Morning (Job 38:7)
At Christ's Coming (Luke 2:13)
For a Sinner's Conversion (Luke 15:10)

202   Continual Occupation

Continual Prayer (Acts 6:4; Col. 4:2)
Continual Praise (Ps. 34:1, with Heb. 13:15)
Continual Service (Dan. 6:16-20)

203   Abiding in Christ

For Fruitfulness (John 15:4-5)
For Prayer (John 15:7)
For Confidence (1 John 2:28)
For Holiness of Walk (1 John 3:16)

How to Abide (John 6:56; 1 John 2:24-27)

204   "Ready"

To Hear (Eccl. 5:1)—Discipleship
To Do (2 Sam. 15:15)—Service
To Preach (Rom. 1:15)—Testimony
To Die (Acts 21:13)—Devotedness

This order is the true path of Christian life and testimony.

205   Instruments of Divine Discipline

The Word (2 Tim. 3:16)—For Correction and Instruction
The Knife (John 15:2)—For Pruning and Fruitfulness
The Thorn (2 Cor. 12:7)—For Prevention and Power
The Rod (Heb. 12:5-7)—For Chastisement and Punishment

206   "No Difference"

In Sin and Need (Rom. 3:22)
In Salvation and Acceptance (Rom. 10:12)
In Standing and Liberty (Acts 15:9)

207   Triune Love

The Love of God (Rom. 5:8)
The Love of Christ (Rom. 8:35)
The Love of the Spirit (Rom. 15:30)

208   Three Good Men

A Good Man (Acts 11:24)—Right with God
A Good Minister (1 Tim. 4:6)—Ready for God
A Good Steward (1 Peter 4:10)—True to God

209   Three Great Truths
In the Epistle to the Romans

No Condemnation, in Christ (Rom. 8:1)
No Separation, from Christ (Rom. 8:35)
No Reservation, for Christ (Rom. 12:1)

210   "His Own Blood"

For our Purchase (Acts 20:28)
For our Loosing from Sin (Rev. 1:5)
For our Sanctification (Heb. 13:12)

211   Emblems of the Holy Spirit

Wind (Acts 2:2; John 3:8)—To Awaken
Breath (Ezek. 37)—To give Life
Water (Ezek. 47:2-13)—To Cleanse and Heal
Oil (Ps. 23:5; 1 John 2:20)—To Anoint and Enlighten

212   Seven "One Anothers"
Which produce and maintain true "fellowship one with another"

Receive one another (Rom. 15:7)
Esteem one another (Phil. 2:3)
Consider one another (Heb. 10:24)
Edify one another (Rom. 14:19)
Exhort one another (Heb. 3:13)
Admonish one another (Rom. 15:14)
Submit to one another (Eph. 5:21)

213 "To the Lord"

Turned to the Lord (Acts 9:35)—Conversion
Added to the Lord (Acts 5:14)—Fellowship
Living to the Lord (Rom. 14:8)—Devotion
Cleaving unto the Lord (Acts 11:23)—Discipleship
Making melody to the Lord (Col. 3:16)—Worship
Doing it heartily to the Lord (Col. 3:23)—Service

214 The Believer Has in Heaven:

A Savior (Phil. 3:20)
An Inheritance (1 Peter 1:4)
His Name written there (Luke 10:20)
His Citizenship is there (Phil. 3:20)
His Hope laid up (Col. 1:5)
His Master is there (Eph. 6:9)
His Home is there (Heb. 11:16)

215 A Threefold Ministry

Wooing and Winning (Prov. 11:30)—The Evangelist
Watering and Watching (Heb. 13:17)—The Pastor
Witnessing to and Warning (Col. 1:28)—The Teacher

216 What God Is Able to Do

Able to Save (Heb. 7:25)
Able to Keep (2 Tim. 1:12)
Able to Deliver (Dan. 3:17)
Able to Succor (Heb. 2:18)
Able to Subdue (Phil. 3:21)

217 Our God

God *for* us (Rom. 8:31)—Justifying
God *with* us (Gen. 28:15)—Keeping
God *in* us (1 John 4:16)—Indwelling

218   Christ's Threefold Headship

Head of Creation (Col. 1:15-17)—Eternally
Head of Every Man (1 Cor. 11:3)—Federally
Head of His Body (Col. 1:18)—Vitally

219   Abiding in Christ

We bear much fruit (John 15:5)
We do not actively sin (1 John 3:6)
We await His coming (1 John 2:28)

220   Things to "Hold Fast"

The Name (Rev. 2:13)
The Word (Titus 1:9)
The Hope (Heb. 10:23)
That which is good (1 Thess. 5:21)
  How?—"In Faith and Love" (2 Tim. 1:13)
  How Long?—"Till I Come" (Rev. 2:25)

221   The Christian's Hope

is not the uncertain thing of men, but the well-grounded
expectation of that which God hath prepared for and
promised to His people.

It is Christ in them (Col. 1:27)

A Good Hope (2 Thess. 2:16)
A Living Hope (1 Peter 1:3)
A Purifying Hope (1 John 3:3)
A Blessed Hope (Titus 2:13)

222   The Seal and Earnest

The Seal (Eph. 2:13)—Securing Believers for Heaven
The Earnest (Eph. 1:14)—Ensuring Heaven to them

   The former marks God's claim on them; the latter
their claim on God.

223   All Things

In Relation to the Lord Jesus

He is *before* all things (Col. 1:17)
By Whom are all things (Heb. 2:10)
For Whom are all things (Heb. 2:10)
Heir of all things (Heb. 1:2)
Preeminent in all things (Col. 1:18)
He will *fill* all things (Eph. 4:10)

224   Three Great Facts

In Ephesians, Chapter 1

Chosen by God, the Father (v. 4)
Redeemed by God, the Son (v. 7)
Sealed by God, the Spirit (v. 13)

225   In Christ Jesus

The believer has

Salvation (2 Tim. 2:10)
Sanctification (1 Cor. 1:2)
Preservation (Jude 1)
Glorification (2 Thess. 1:12)

226   The Church in Three Aspects

A Building (Eph. 2:20-21)—Christ, the Foundation
A Body (Eph. 4:15-16)—Christ, the Head
A Bride (Eph. 5:25-32)—Christ, the Bridegroom

227   Sowing

What to Sow—"Precious Seed" (Ps. 126:6)
How to Sow—"In Tears" (Ps. 126:6)
Where to Sow—"Beside all Waters" (Isa. 32:20)
When to Sow—"Morning," "Evening," always (Eccl. 11:6)

228   "Before the Foundation"

The Son, beloved of the Father (John 17:24)
The Lamb, foreordained to die (1 Peter 1:20)
The Church, chosen in Christ (Eph. 1:4)

229   Three Great Truths

(1 Peter 1)

Redemption gives a New Owner (v. 18)
Resurrection brings to a New Position (v. 19)
Regeneration imparts a New Life (v. 23)

230   Three Graces

(1 Thessalonians 1)

"Work of *Faith*" (v. 3)—Turned to God (v. 9)
"Labor of *Love*" (v. 3)—Serve the Living God (v. 9)
"Patience of *Hope*" (v. 3)—Wait for the Son (v. 10)

231   Three Classes of Workers

(Nehemiah 3)

"Who put not their necks" (v. 5)—Honorary
"Who repaired the wall" (v. 6)—Practical
"Who repaired earnestly" (v. 20)—Devoted

232   The Believer's Place and Portion

On His Shoulder (Luke 15:5)—Our Salvation
In His Hand (John 10:28)—Our Security
At His Feet (Luke 10:39)—For Teaching
On His Bosom (John 13)—In Communion

233   Continuing

Continue in the Grace of God (Acts 13:43)
Continue in the Faith (Acts 14:22)
Continue in the Things Learned (1 Tim. 3:14)
Continue in the Love of Christ (John 15:9)
Continue in Prayer (Col. 4:2)

234   The Christian in Varied Aspects

A Child in *Relationship* (1 John 3:1)
A Saint in *Separation* (Rom. 1:7)
A Priest in *Nearness* (1 Peter 3:5)
A Steward in *Responsibility* (1 Peter 5:10)
A Witness in *Testimony* (Acts 26:16)

235   Present Blessings

Now, justified by His blood (Rom. 5:8)—Justification
Now, delivered from the law (Rom. 7:6)—Deliverance
Now, no condemnation (Rom. 8:1)—Freedom
Now, made nigh (Eph. 2:13)—Nearness
Now, the sons of God (1 John 3:1)—Sonship

236   The False

The Devil's Counterfeits of God's Realities

False Christs (Matt. 24:24, with 1 John 2:18)
False Apostles (Rev. 2:2, with 2 Cor. 11:13)
False Teachers (2 Peter 2:1, with 2 Tim. 3:8)
False Brethren (Gal. 2:4, with 2 Cor. 11:26)

237   The Hope of the Believer

A Living Hope (1 Peter 1:3)
A Good Hope (2 Thess. 2:16)
A Blessed Hope (Titus 2:13)
A Purifying Hope (1 John 3:3)

238 Full Assurance

Full Assurance of Faith (Heb. 10:22)
Full Assurance of Understanding (Heb. 6:11)
Full Assurance of Hope (Col. 2:2)

Faith rests in Christ's finished work—Past
Understanding learns Christ's place—Present
Hope looks onward to Christ's glory—Future

239 Good Things for God's People

To draw near to God (Ps. 73:28)
To give thanks (Ps. 92:1)
To bear the yoke (Lam. 3:27)
To be afflicted (Ps. 119:71)
To be zealously affected (Gal. 4:8)

240 God and Father

To Christ (John 20:17; 1 Peter 1:3; Eph. 3:14)
To Christians (Eph. 4:6; Gal. 4:6; Eph. 1:17)

In these two great relationships does God stand to Christ, and to us, and such are the names by which saints should address Him.

241 God and His People

God *for* His people (Rom. 8:31)—Saving
God *with* His people (Gen. 33:15)—Keeping
God *in* His people (2 Cor. 6:16)—Dwelling

242 A Fourfold Relation to Christ

My Sheep (John 10:27)—In Security
My Disciples (John 15:8)—In Obedience
My Friends (John 15:14)—In Communion
My Brethren (John 20:17)—In Relationship

243 The Bible

"The Holy Scriptures" (2 Tim. 3:15)—Divine Inspiration
"The Oracles of God" (Rom. 3:2)—Divine Authority
"The Word of God" (Matt. 7:36)—Divine Revelation

244 God Manifested in Christ

"God was manifest in the flesh" (1 Tim. 3:16)

The Word of Life (1 John 1)—God Heard
The Light of Life (John 8:12)—God Seen
The Fulness of Life (John 10:10)—God Enjoyed

245 Paul's Five Faithful Sayings

Salvation (1 Tim. 1:15)
Service (1 Tim. 3:1)
Suffering (1 Tim. 4:7)
Recompence (2 Tim. 2:11)
Testimony (Titus 3:8)

246 The Inheritance and the Heirs

The Saints' inheritance prepared for them (1 Peter 1:4)
The Saints made meet for the inheritance (Col. 1:12)

247 Tears

Tears of Faith (Mark 9:24)
Tears of Devotion (Luke 7:38)
Tears of Service (Acts 20:19)
Tears of Sympathy (2 Tim. 1:4)
Tears of Warning (Acts 20:31)

248 The Word of God

Converts (Ps. 19:7)—The Soul
Enlightens (Ps. 19:8)—The Eyes
Cleanses (Ps. 119:9)—The Ways

249   Paul's Growth
In Three Stages, at Three Dates

A.D.59—The least of the Apostles (1 Cor. 15:9)
A.D.64—Less than the least of Saints (Eph. 3:8)
A.D.66—The chief of Sinners (1 Tim. 1:1:5)

250   The Believer's Standing

Standing in Grace (Rom. 5:2)
Standing by Faith (2 Cor. 1:24)
Standing fast in Liberty (Gal. 5:1)
Standing in Armor of God (Eph. 6:11)

251   Christ Set Down
As described in the Epistle to the Hebrews

As Sin Purger (Heb. 1)
As Great High Priest (Heb. 8:1)
As Perfecter of Faith (Heb. 12:2)

252   Christ, the Fulness

The Father's Pleasing (Col. 1:19)
In Christ all fulness dwells (Col. 2:9)
Of His fulness we received (John 1:16)
The Church, the fulness of Christ (Eph. 1:23)

253   Three Deaths
In which all believers share, true of all judicially in Christ,
actually to faith

Dead to the Law (Rom. 7:4)
Dead to the World (Col. 2:20)
Dead to Sin (Rom. 6:2)

254 Three Stages of Progress in Communion

As set forth in the Song of Solomon
(Daniel 1:1-4:37)

"My Beloved is Mine and I am His" (2:16)
"I am My Beloved's and My Beloved is Mine" (6:13)
"I am My Beloved's, His desire toward Me" (7:10)

The *First* is what I have in Him—Foremost
The *Second* is what He has in me—First
The *Third* is, Him only—Mine forgotten

255 Threefold Cleansing

Our Consciences (Heb. 10:2-22)—By the Blood
Our Ways (Ps. 119:9)—By the Word
Ourselves (2 Cor. 7:1)—By Separation

256 Three Favored Disciples

Peter, James, and John, thrice taken by the Lord apart

To See His Power (Mark 5:37)—In Jairus' House
To Share His Sorrow (Mark 14:33)—In the Garden
To Behold His Glory (Mark 9:2)—On the Mount

257 "In My Name"

Salvation in My Name (Acts 4:12)
Service in My Name (Mark 9:41)
Praying in My Name (John 14:13)
Gathering in My Name (Matt. 18:20)
Holding Fast My Name (Rev. 2:13)

258 Following the Lord

Obediently as a Sheep (John 10:27)
Devotedly as a Servant (John 12:26)
Patiently as a Sufferer (1 Peter 2:21)

259   **Christ Manifested**

As Set Forth in John's First Epistle

Manifested as the Life (1 John 1:2)—In His Life
Manifested to take away sins (1 John 3:5)—In His Death
Manifested in Glory (1 John 3:2)—At His Appearing

The word in each case is the same, and occurs nine times in 1 John.

260   **God's Fourfold Testimony to Christ**

God Anointed Him (Acts 10:38)—At His Baptism
God was with Him (Acts 10:38)—In His Service
God raised Him (Acts 13:30)—From the Grave
God ordained Him (Acts 17:31)—As the Judge

261   **A Sevenfold View of the Spirit's Work**

As Seen in Ephesians

The Seal of the Spirit (Eph. 1:13)
The Earnest of the Spirit (Eph. 1:14)
The Revealing of the Spirit (Eph. 1:17)
Access by the Spirit (Eph. 2:18)
Strength of the Spirit (Eph. 3:16)
Fulness of the Spirit (Eph. 5:18)
Praying in the Spirit (Eph. 6:17)

262   **Three "Togethers"**

For all Servants of Christ

Praying Together (Acts 3:1)—One Desire
Working Together (2 Cor. 6:1)—One Master
Striving together (Phil. 1:27)—One Aim

263 Eternal Life

In Three Different Aspects

A Promise (Titus 1:4)—Past
A Possession (1 John 5:9)—Present
A Prospect (Rom. 6:22)—Future

264 The Word Applied Daily

To Search the Inner Man (Heb. 4:12)
To Sanctify the Outward Walk (John 17:17)
To Cleanse the Way (Ps. 119:9)
To Feed the New Life (1 Peter 2:2)

265 The Work of Grace in the Believer

As shown in the Philippian Epistle

The Work Begun (Phil. 1:6)—Inauguration
The Work Progressing (Phil. 2:13)—Progression
The Work Completed (Phil. 3:21)—Consummation

266 Three Fundamental Truths

(Hebrews 10)

The Will of God (v. 7)—The Source
The Work of Christ (v. 10)—The Cause
The Witness of the Spirit (v. 15)—The Seal

267 The Lord's Body

Prepared by the Father (Heb. 10:5)
Taken at Incarnation (Heb. 2:14)
Offered at Calvary (Heb. 10:10)
Buried in the Tomb (John 19:40)
Handled in Resurrection (Luke 24:39)
Glorified at Ascension (Phil. 3:21)
Discerned in Communion (1 Cor. 11:29)

268   Christ's Service for the Church

In Seven Particulars (Eph. 5:25-27)

He Loved the Church ⎫ He gave Himself ⎬	Past; At the Cross.
He Sanctifies ⎫ He Cleanses ⎬ He Nourishes ⎭ He Cherishes	Present: On the Throne.
He will Present ⎬	Future: At Its Coming.

269   Threefold Cords

In which the Names of the Three Persons of the Godhead appear

In Atonement (Heb. 9:14)
In Resurrection (Rom. 8:11)
In Regeneration (John 1:12; 1 John 5:1; John 3:5)
In Prayer (Rom. 8:27)
In Union (Eph. 2:22)

270   Preparation for Service

Of the Servant (2 Tim. 2:21; Exod. 35:30, 35, 36)
Of the Heart (Ezra 7:10; 1 Sam. 8:3)
Of the Message (Eccl. 12:10, with 2 Tim. 3:18)

271   In Adam and in Christ

By our connection in nature with Adam, we inherit the sin; by union with Christ through grace we receive the grace.

In Adam	In Christ
Sin (Rom. 5:12)	Righteousness (2 Cor. 5:21)
Condemnation (Rom. 5:19)	Justification (Rom. 4:25)
Death (Rom. 5:23)	Life (1 John 5:11)

272   The Christian Warrior

And his panoply in Ephesians 6:13-18

Girdle of Truth (Eph. 14, with Ps. 51:6; Col. 3:16)
Breastplate of Righteousness (Eph. 6:14, with Prov. 28:1)
Sandals of Peace (Eph. 6:15; Rom. 5:1; 10:15)
Shield of the Faith (Eph. 6:16; Ps. 91:4; Jude 3)
Helmet of Salvation (Eph. 6:16; Ps. 27:1; Eph. 2:8)
Sword of the Spirit (Eph. 6:17; Heb. 4:12; Matt. 4:7)

273   Spiritual Hygiene

Pure Milk (1 Peter 2:2; Heb. 5:13)
Healthy Food (1 Tim. 6:3; 4:6)
Strict Cleanliness (Ps. 119:9; Eph. 5:26)
Plenty of Exercise (1 Tim. 4:7; Heb. 12:11)

274   What Christ Does for His People

He Quickens them (John 5:25)—As the Life Giver
He Saves them (Matt. 1:21)—As the Savior
He Seals them (Eph. 1:13)—As the Owner
He Leads them (John 10:27)—As the Shepherd
He Succors them (Heb. 2)—As the Priest
He Restores them (1 John 2:1)—As the Advocate
He Comes for them (John 14:3)—As the Bridegroom

275   Seven Togethers With Christ

Which bind the Saints indissolubly to Him

Crucified Together (Rom. 6:5-6; Gal. 2:20)
Buried Together (Rom. 6:4; Col. 2:12)
Quickened Together (Eph. 2:5; Col. 2:13)
Raised Together (Eph. 2:6; Col. 3:1)
Seated Together (Eph. 2:6; Rev. 4:4)
Sufferers Together (Rom. 8:17; 1 Peter 4:13)
Glorified Together (Rom. 8:18; 2 Tim. 2:12)

276 **"The Faith"**

Once grace delivered to the Saints (Jude 3)

One newly come to the Faith (1 Tim. 3:6)
One weak in the Faith (Rom. 14:1)
One who kept (guarded) the Faith (2 Tim. 4:7)
Some who erred from the Faith (1 Tim. 6:21)
Some depart from the Faith (1 Tim. 4:1)
Some deny the Faith (1 Tim. 5:8)
Some overthrow the Faith (2 Tim 2:18)

277 **Scriptural Arithmetic**

As Exemplified in the Early Church

Addition—Three Thousand Added (Acts 2:41)
Subtraction—Two Taken Away (Acts 5:1-10)
Multiplication—Disciples Multiplied (Acts 6:1)
Division—Scattered Abroad (Acts 8:1)

278 **Joy**

In Christ (John 15:11)
In the Spirit (Rom. 14:17)
In God (Rom. 5:11)

279 **Seven Links With the Lord**

Knowing the Lord (Heb. 8:11)
Confessing the Lord (Rom. 10:9)
Following the Lord (Josh. 14:8)
Serving the Lord (Acts 20:19)
Honoring the Lord (Prov. 3:9)
Magnifying the Lord (Ps. 34:3)
Present with the Lord (2 Cor. 5:8)

280 God's Attributes Toward Us

Mercy shown toward us (Ps. 86:13)
Kindness manifested toward us (Eph. 2:7)
Love commended toward us (Rom. 5:8)
Grace abounding toward us (2 Cor. 9:8)

281 God's First Things

Seek ye *first* the Kingdom of God (Matt. 6:33)
Cleanse *first* that which is within (Matt. 23:26)
First cast out the beam out of thine own eye (Matt. 6:6)
Learn *first* to show piety at home (1 Tim. 5:4)
Judgment must *first* begin at house of God (1 Peter 4:17)

282 Christ, the Living One

The Living *Stone* on which we *build* (1 Peter 2:5)
The Living *Bread* on which we *feed* (John 6:51)
The Living *Way* by which we draw *near* (Heb. 10:20)
The Living *Priest* through whom we *worship* (Heb. 13:25)
The Living *Hope* for which we *wait* (Peter 1:3)

283 Good Works

The Believer in Christ is

Created unto good works (Eph. 2:10)
Furnished unto all good works (2 Tim. 3:17)
Careful to maintain good works (Titus 3:8)
Prepared unto every good work (2 Tim. 2:21)
Zealous of good works (Titus 2:14)
Rich in good works (1 Tim. 6:18)
A Pattern in good works (Titus 2:7)

284 The Lord's Death

As described by Himself

For the Sheep (John 10:11)
For the Many (Matt. 20:28)
For the World (John 6:51)

285 Symbols of the Word

A *Mirror* to show us ourselves (James 1:23)
A *Hammer* to break the will (Jer. 23:29)
A *Fire* to melt the heart (Jer. 23:29)
A *Sword* to pierce the conscience (Heb. 4:12)
A *Seed* to quicken the soul (1 Peter 1:23)
A *Laver* to cleanse the way (Eph. 5:26)
A *Light* to show the path (Ps. 119:105)

286 Characteristics of God's Word

The Word of Life (Phil. 2:16)—To be Held Forth
The Word of Reconciliation (2 Cor. 5:19)—To be Proclaimed
The Word of Salvation (Acts 28:26)—To be Heard
The Word of Truth (Eph. 1:13)—To be Received
The Word of Faith (Rom. 10:8)—To be Believed
The Word of Wisdom (1 Cor. 12:8)—To be Ministered
The Word of Faithfulness (Titus 1:9)—To be Held Fast

287 Threefold Peace

Perfect Peace (Isa. 26:3)
Abundant Peace (Jer. 30:6)
Peace passing all understanding (Phil. 4:7)

288 The Believer's Offerings

His Body (Rom. 12:1)—Acceptable
His Praises (Heb. 13:15)—Well Pleasing
His Gifts (Phil. 4:18)—Sweet Smelling

289   Christh, the Deliverer

(Read Romans 11:26; Luke 1:74; 4:18)

He delivers all His people from—

The Lowest Hell (Ps. 84:12; Rev. 20:15)
The Wrath to Come (1 Thess. 1:10; Rom. 8:1)
The Power of Darkness (Col. 1:13; 1 Peter 2:9)
The Curse of Law (Rom. 7:6; Gal. 2:19)
The Present World (Gal. 1:3; John 17:16)
The Power of Evil (2 Tim. 3:11; 4:17)
The Presence of Sin (Rom. 8:21; 1 John 3:2)

290   Our Great High Priest

Called in Resurrection (Heb. 5:7, with Acts 13:33)
Acting in Heaven (Heb. 4:4; 8:1; 9:24)
Character and Work (Heb. 2:17; 4:15; 7:26)
Order and Dignity (Heb. 6:20; 7:4, 17, 24, 28)

291   The Power of Love

Drawn by Love (Jer. 31:3)—In Conversion
Satisfied by Love (Song of Sol. 2:4)—In Communion
Constrained by Love (2 Cor. 5:14)—In Consecration
Energized by Love (Phil. 1:17)—In Confession

292   The Blood of Christ

Procures for Believers

Remission of sin (Matt. 26:28; Acts 10:38)
Reconciliation to God (Col. 1:20; 2 Cor. 5:21)
Redemption from bondage (Eph. 1:7; 1 Peter 1:19)
Justification from sin (Rom. 5:9; 3:25)
Nearness to God (Eph. 2:13; Heb. 10:19)
Fitness for Heaven (Rev. 7:14; 5:9)

293   Christ in His People

Christ liveth in me (Gal. 2:20)—Their Life
Christ dwelling in them (Eph. 3:17)—Their Strength
Christ in you, the Hope (Col. 1:27)—Their Hope

294   Fruits of Regeneration

Love to God and His people (1 John 5:2; 4:7)
Victory over the World (1 John 5:4; 2:16)
Doth not practice sin (1 John 3:9; 5:18)
Lives a righteous life (1 John 2:29)

295   Four Views of Christ

The Son of God (John 1:49; 20:31)
The Son of Man (Luke 9:22; 19:10)
The Sacrifice for Sin (Heb. 9:22; 10:12)
The Savior of Sinners (1 Tim. 1:15; Rom. 5:8)

296   Four Views of Man

Created in God's Image (Gen. 1:27; Eccl. 7:29)
Ruined by Sin (Rom. 5:12; Rom. 3:12)
Regenerated by the Spirit (John 3:7; Eph. 4:24)
Conformed to Christ (Rom. 8:29; 2 Thess. 1:10)

297   Three Great Realities

Sin has ruined all (Rom. 3:23)
Christ has ransomed all (1 Tim. 2:6)
Faith saves all (Acts 13:39)

298   The Name of Jesus

The Power to Save (Matt. 1:21)
The Channel of Life (John 20:31)
The Means of Remission (Acts 10:43)
The Center of Gathering (Matt. 18:20)

299   Three Relationships
In John's Gospel

"My Sheep" (John 10:14)—Christ, the Shepherd
"My Friends" (John 15:14)—Christ, the Lover
"My Brethren" (John 20:17)—Christ, the Firstborn

300   Living

The Living God (1 Thess. 1:9)—To Serve
The Living Christ (1 Peter 2:5)—To Come to
The Living Word (Heb. 4:12)—To Search us
The Living Bread (John 6:51)—To Feed on
The Living Way (Heb. 10:20)—To Draw Near by
The Living Water (John 4:10)—To Drink
The Living Sacrifice (Rom. 12:1)—To Offer

301   Two Classes to "Mark"

"Mark them which so walk" (Phil. 3:17)
"Mark them that cause divisions" (Rom. 16:17-18)
The former are godly *walkers*; the latter godless *talkers*

302   The Bodies of Christ

The Body of His Flesh (Col. 1:22)—Christ Human
The Body of His Glory (Phil. 3:21)—Christ Glorified
His Body, the Church (Col. 1:18)—Christ Mystical

303   The Christian Calling
In its Threefold Character

A High Calling (Phil. 3:14, with 1 Sam. 1:8)
A Heavenly Calling (Heb. 3:1, with Eph. 1:3)
A Holy Calling (2 Tim. 1:9, with 1 Peter 1:15)

304   The Christian's Race

Running after Christ (Song of Sol. 1:4)
Running in His Way (Ps. 119:32)
Running with Patience (Heb. 12:1)
Running, not uncertainly (1 Cor.9:26)
Running, yet not weary (Isa. 40:31)
Running, looking unto Jesus (Heb. 12:2)

305   Seeing Jesus

"We *would* see Jesus" (John 12:21)—An Earnest Desire
"We *do* see Jesus" (Heb. 2:9)—An Open Vision
"We *shall* see Jesus" (1 John 3:2)—A Bright Prospect

306   Rejoicings

God, the Father rejoicing (Zeph. 3:17)
God, the Son rejoicing (Luke 15:6)
The Church rejoicing (Acts 15:3)
The Servant rejoicing (Phil. 4:10)
The Saved Sinner rejoicing (Luke 15:24)

307   Things to Learn

For all Young Believers

Learn of Christ (Matt. 11:28)—Inner Life
Learn to keep the Word (Ps. 119:71)—Social Life
Learn to show Piety (1 Tim. 5:4)—Home Life
Learn to do Well (Isa. 1:17)—Church Life
Learn to maintain Good Works (Titus 3:14)—World Life

308 The Christian's Place in the World

As a Saint (John 17:16)—In Separation from it
As a Subject (Rom. 13:1)—In Subjection to it
As a Servant (John 20:21)—In Service toward it

309   Keeping

Keep thine heart (Prov. 4:23)
Keep thyself pure (1 Tim. 5:22)
Keep yourselves unspotted (James 1:27)
Keep yourselves in the Love of God (Jude 21)

310   The Kingdom of God
A Spiritual Sphere, Created and Governed by God

Natural Man cannot see or enter it (John 3:3-5; 1 Cor. 6:9)
Its Origin, through the Word (Mark 4:26; 1 Peter 1:23)
Its Character and Development (Rom. 14:17; 1 Cor. 4:20)
To be Sought after First (Matt. 6:23; Acts 14:22)
True Ministry furthers it (Acts 20:25; 28:23; Col. 4:11)

311   The Heart and its Inmates

The Heart in Nature (Jer. 17:9-10; Matt. 15:18)
The Heart at Conversion (2 Cor. 4:6; Acts 16:14; Rom. 10:9)
The Heart's New Dwellers (Gal. 4:6; Eph. 3:17; Ps. 119:11)
The Heart's New Motive (Rom. 5:4; 1 Peter 1:22; Matt. 12:35)
The Heart's New Condition (Heb. 10:22; Matt. 5:8; Eph. 5:19)

312   Three Appearings of Christ
(Hebrews 9:24-28)

"He once appeared" (v.26)—Atonement
"He now appears" (v. 24)—Advocacy
"He shall appear" (v. 28)—Advent

313   Two Periods

"Latter Times" (1 Tim. 4:1)—Romanism and Ritual
"Last Days" (2 Tim. 3:1)—Rationalism and Religion

314   Disciples of Christ

The Gospel's Object (Matt. 33:18)—"Make Disciples"
The Apostles' Practice (Acts 14:21)—"They made Disciples"
The True Marks (John 13:35; Luke 14:26)—Love, Obedience
The Plain Path (Matt. 10:24-25; Luke 14:27)—Rejection

315   The Love of Christ

To His Father (John 14:31, with Exod. 21:5)
To His Church (Eph. 5:25; Rev. 3:9)
To His Saints (Rev. 1:5; John 11:5)
To the Individual (Gal. 2:20; John 14:23)

316   Gathering

Gathering to Christ, by the Gospel (John 12:32)
Gathering to Christ, in the Church (Matt. 18:20)
Gathering to Christ, at His Coming (2 Thess. 2:1)

317   Three Fellowships

The Fellowship of Life (1 John 1:2-3)
The Fellowship of Light (1 John 1:7)
The Fellowship of Labor (Phil. 4:3)

318   "The Saints"

Saints called by Grace (Rom. 1:7)
Saints gathered to Christ (Ps. 50:5)
Saints in Assembly (Ps. 89:7)
Saints faithfully Ruled (Hos. 11:12)
Saints glorified with Christ (2 Thess. 1:10)

319   The Believer's Justification

The *Source* of Justification (Rom. 8:33)—God
The *Principle* of Justification (Rom. 3:24)—Grace
The *Cause* of Justification (Rom. 5:8)—Blood
The *Way* of Justification (Rom. 5:1)—Faith
The *Proof* of Justification (James 2:18)—Works

320   The Death of Christ
In Seven Aspects

A Death of Shame (Heb. 12:2; Isa. 50:6; Mark 14:65)
A Death of Suffering (Luke 22:15; Heb. 2:9-10)
A Martyr's Death (1 Peter 2:21; Acts 2:23; 13:28)
A Sacrificial Death (Heb. 9:14; Eph. 5:2; Heb. 9:26)
A Sin-bearing Death (1 Peter 2:24; Isa. 53:6; John 1:29)
A Voluntary Death (John 10:18; 18:8-11; 19:30)
An All-sufficient Death (John 19:30; Heb. 1:2; Isa. 42:21)

321   The Taker-away of Sin
(John 1:29)

By Sacrifice (Heb. 9:26)—From Before God
By Salvation (Matt. 1:21)—From His People
By Sanctification (1 John 3:9)—In His Saints

322   Four Attitudes of Believers
As seen at the Close of the Four Gospels

As Worshipers *of* Christ (Matt. 28:9)
As Workers *with* Christ (Mark 16:19)
As Witnesses *to* Christ (Luke 24:47)
As Waitees *for* Christ (John 16:22)

323 The Christian's Race

The Start (Heb. 12:1)—Conversion and Stripping
The Course (1 Cor. 9:24)—From the Cross to Glory
The Goal (Phil. 3:12)—Christ in Glory
The Reward (2 Tim. 4:8; 1 Cor. 9:25)—A Crown

324 Christ Is All

As Sacrifice (Heb. 10:12-18)—No Romanism
As Priest (Heb. 8:1)—No Ritualism
As Lord (1 Cor. 8:7)—No Lawlessness
As Head (Col. 2:19)—No Clerisy
As Object (Phil. 3:14)—No Worldliness

325 Vessels

Marred in the Fall (Jer. 18:3-4, with Eph. 2:10)
Chosen by Grace (Acts 9:15; Eph. 1:4)
Prepared for Glory (Rom. 9:23; Rev. 21:11)
Fitted for Service (2 Tim. 2:21; 3:17)

326 Three Aspects of the Holy Spirit's Work

Regenerating (John 3:5, with Titus 3:5)
Indwelling (John 4:14, with Rom. 8:14-15)
Outflowing (John 7:38, with Gal. 3:5)

327 Christian Earnestness

Give earnest heed to the Word (Heb. 2:1)
Earnestly contend for the Faith (Jude 3)
Earnestly pray to God (Luke 22:24; James 5:17)
Earnest care for saints (2 Cor. 7:7)
Earnest longing for glory (2 Cor. 5:2)

328   Meekness

Receive the Word with meekness (James 1:21)—Inwardly
Be clothed with meekness (Col. 3:12)—Outwardly
A meek and quiet spirit (1 Peter 3:4)—Manifestly
Restoring the erring with meekness (Gal. 5:1)—In Service
Answer every man in meekness (1 Peter 3:15)—In Testimony

329   Four Links With Christ

In the Epistle to the Colossians
Quickened with Christ (Col. 2:13)
Risen with Christ (Col. 3:1)
Hid with Christ (Col. 3:3)
Appearing with Christ (Col. 3:4)

330   God's Little Things

A Little Flock (Luke 12:32)—To Care for
A Little Strength (Rev. 3:8)—To Serve
A Little While (Heb. 10:37)—To Wait

331   "Go's" of Christ

Go and *Sell* (Mark 10:21)—To the Rich one
God and *Tell* (Mark 5:19)—To the Saved one
Go and *Show* (Luke 17:14)—To the Cleansed one
Go and *Teach* (Matt. 28:18)—To the Sent one

332   Christian Postures

Sitting as a Learner (Luke 10:39)
Kneeling as a Suppliant (Acts 20:36)
Leaning as a Weakling (Song of Sol. 8:5)
Standing as a Warrior (Eph. 6:14)
Running as a Racer (Heb. 12:1)

333   Objects to Consider

In the Epistle to the Hebrews

Consider the Apostle and High Priest (Heb. 3:1)
Consider Him who endured (Heb. 12:3)
Consider one another (Heb. 10:24)

334   A Threefold Work of the Spirit

Described in Romans 8

The Spirit of Life (v. 2)—Giving Freedom
The Spirit of Sonship (v. 14)—Giving Guidance
The Spirit of Intercession (v. 26)—Giving Help

335   Three Crucifixions

(Galatians 6:14-16)

Of Christ—"The Cross of our Lord Jesus"
Of the World—"The World Crucified to Me"
Of Self—"I to the World"

336   Things Everlasting

The Present Possession of All Believers

Everlasting Love (Jer. 31:3)
Everlasting Life (John 6:47)
Everlasting Salvation (Isa. 45:17)
Everlasting Strength (Isa. 26:4)

337   The Presence of the Lord

Is Intolerable to the Sinner (Gen. 3:8; 4:16)
Is Salvation to the Saint (Ps. 42:5; 31:8)
Is Rest to the Servant (Exod. 33:14-15)

338   Three Kinds of Giving

Thanksgiving (Eph. 5:20; Heb. 13:15)
Substance-giving (2 Cor. 9:7; Heb. 13:16)
Self-giving (2 Cor. 8:5; Rom. 6:13)

339   Seven Aspects of Christian Life

(2 Timothy 2)

A Son (v. 1)—In Affection
A Steward (v. 2)—In Faithfulness
A Soldier (v. 2)—In Endurance
A Wrestler (v. 5)—In Skill
A Workman (v. 15)—In Diligence
A Vessel (v. 21)—In Fitness
A Servant (v. 24)—In Obedience

340   "In Love"

Walking in Love (Eph. 5:2)
Acting in Love (Eph. 4:2)
Speaking in Love (Eph. 4:2)

341 Three Requests of the Lord Jesus

"Watch with Me" (Mark 12:37)
"Remember Me" (1 Cor. 11:24)
"Follow Me" (John 21:19)

342   Three States of the Believer

(2 Corinthians 5:1-8)

In our "Earthly House" (v. 1)—The Present State
"Unclothed" (v. 4)—The Intermediate State
"Clothed upon" (v. 2)—The Eternal State

343   Names Given to God's People in "Acts"

Believers (Acts 5:14)—In Faith
Brethren (Acts 6:3)—In Love
Disciples (Acts 9:1)—In Obedience
Saints (Acts 9:3)—In Separation
Christians (Acts 11:26)—In Testimony

344   Christian Liberality

How to Give (2 Cor. 9:7; Rom. 12:8)
When to Give (1 Cor. 16:2; 2 Cor. 9:5)
What to Give (1 Cor. 9:7; 1 Peter 4:11)
To Whom to Give (3 John 5-8; Gal. 6:6)

345   Enduring Hardness

(2 Timothy)
[The Greek Word is the same in each case]

Endure Hardness, in the Gospel (2 Tim. 1:8)
Endure Hardness, as a Soldier (2 Tim. 2:3)
Endure Hardness, unto Bonds (2 Tim. 2:9)
Endure Hardness, as an Evangelist (2 Tim. 4:5)

346   Three Great Foes

The World (James 4:4)—Around us
The Flesh (Gal. 5:17)—Within us
The Devil (Eph. 6:11-12)—Above us

347   Prayer, Praise, Worship

In *Prayer* we are occupied with our *Needs* (Mark 11:24)
In *Praise* we are rejoicing in our *Fulness* (Ps. 52:9)
In Worship we are occupied with our *God* (John 4:24)

348 Acceptable Service

Serve with all thine heart (Deut. 10:12)
Serve with a willing mind (1 Chron. 28:9)
Serve with all humility (Acts 20:19)
Serve with gladness (Ps. 100:2)

349 Threefold Glory of God

His Creation Glory (Ps. 19:1)—In the Heavens
His Redemption Glory (2 Cor. 4:4)—In Christ Risen
His Eternal Glory (1 Peter 5:10)—In His Saints

350 "For the Name"

Forsaking all for the Name (Matt. 19:29)
Going forth for the Name (3 John 8)
Laboring for the Name (Rev. 2:3)

351 Christ, the Girded Servant

In the Upper Room (John 12:4)—Past
In the Midst of the Churches (Rev. 1:13)—Present
In the Coming glory (Luke 12:37)—Future

352 Spiritual Progress

From Faith to Faith (Rom. 1:7)
From Strength to Strength (Ps. 84:7)
From Glory to Glory (2 Cor. 3:18)

353 Two Washings in John 13:10

"He that is *washed*" washed all over—Once for all
"*Wash* his feet," wash in part—Continuously

The *first* accords with the washing of Regeneration (Titus 3:4)
The *second* with the daily cleansing by the Word (Ps. 119:9)

354   Seal and Earnest of the Spirit

(Ephesians 1:13-14)

God's *Seal*, marking His claim upon us

Our *Earnest*, the pledge and foretaste of Glory

355   Three Leavens

Leaven of Pharisees (Matt. 16:1)—Ritualism

Leaven of Sadducees (Luke 16:11)—Rationalism

Leaven of Herod (Matt. 8:15)—Lawlessness

356   Fruitfulness

"Fruit" (John 15:2)—By Union

"More Fruit" (John 15:2)—By Pruning

"Much Fruit" (John 15:5)—By Abiding

357 Daily Fare for a Weakly Believer

The Roast Lamb (Exod. 12:9)—Christ Crucified

The Daily Manna (Luke 15:23)—Christ Humbled

The Old Corn (Josh. 5:11)—Christ Glorified

New Wine (John 2:10)—Heavenly Joy

Pure Milk (1 Peter 2:2)—The Word

Grapes of Eschol (Num. 13:23)—The Spirit's Earnest

358   "Jesus in the Midst"

Among the Doctors (Luke 2:46)—Hearing

On the Cross (John 19:18)—Suffering

Among the Disciples (John 20:19-29)—Comforting

In the Assembly (Matt. 18:20)—Gathering

Among the Churches (Rev. 1:13)—Judging

In the Glory (Heb. 2:12)—Singing

On the Throne (Rev. 5:6)—Reigning

359   Three "Abides"

"Abide *with* Me" (1 Sam. 22:23)—Safety
"Abide *in* Me" (John 15:4)—Communion
"Abide *for* Me" (Hosea 3:3)—Stewardship

360   Our God

God *Before* us (Deut. 1:30)
God *Behind* us (Isa. 52:12)
God *Above* us (Ps. 18:16)
God *Underneath* us (Deut. 33:27)
God *Around* us (Ps. 125:2)

361   The Christian, a Soldier

His Captain (Heb. 2:10; Josh. 5:14)
His Comrades (Phil. 2:26; Philem. 2)
His Armor (Eph. 6:11-18)
His Enemy (1 Peter 5:8; Eph. 6:12)
His Fight (1 Tim. 6:12; 1:18)

362   Man's History

Man Created in God's Image (Gen. 1:27)
Man Ruined by Sin (Rom. 5:12)
Man Redeemed by Christ (Eph. 1:7)
Man Regenerated by the Spirit (John 3:5)
Man Rejoicing in Hope of Glory (Rom. 5:2)

363   How to Use the Word

Search it (John 5:39; 1 Peter 1:10-11)
Examine it (Acts 17:11; 1 Cor. 2:10-13)
Meditate in it (Ps. 1:2; 119:15)
Delight in it (Ps. 119:47; Jer. 15:17)
Declare it (Ps. 119:13; Jer. 23:28)

364   **Seven "In Whoms"**

In the Epistle to the Ephesians

In whom we have Redemption (Eph. 1:7)
In whom we trusted (Eph. 1:13)
In whom believing we are sealed (Eph. 1:13)
In whom we have an inheritance (Eph. 1:11)
In whom we are builded together (Eph. 2:22)
In whom the building is framed together (Eph. 2:21)
In whom we have access (Eph. 3:12)

365   Three Persons of the Godhead

(Romans 8)

God our Justifier (vv. 31-32)
Christ our Intercessor (vv. 34-35)
The Spirit our Helper (vv. 26-27)

366   Two Pointed Questions

"Who art thou that judgest another?" (James 4:12)
"Who is sufficient for these things?" (2 Cor. 2:16)

367   Two Doors

The Closed Door (Matt. 6:6)—For Prayer
The Opened Door (Rev. 3:8)—For Service

368   "Shall Nots"

True of all Believers in Christ

Shall not perish (John 10:28)
Shall not come into judgment (John 5:24)
Shall not want (Ps. 23:1)
Shall not be afraid (Ps. 112:7)
Shall not walk in darkness (John 8:12)

369 Threefold Victory

Victory over sin (Rom. 6:14-15)—By the Gospel
Victory over Satan (1 John 2:13-14)—By the Word
Victory over the World (1 John 5:4-5)—By Faith

370 Jehovah's Wings

Wings of shelter (Ps. 17:8)
Wings of security (Ps. 91:4)
Wings of support (Deut. 32:11)

371 Tongues

Confounded at Babel (Gen. 11:8)—Judgment
Preaching at Pentecost (Acts 2:6)—Grace
Praising in Heaven (Rev. 5:9)—Glory

372 Christ, the True

As set forth in John's Gospel

The True Light (John 1:9)—Receive Him
The True Bread (John 6:32)—Feed on Him
The True Vine (John 15:1)—Abide in Him

373 Four Attitudes in Ephesians

Seated with Christ (Eph. 2:6)
Kneeling in Prayer (Eph. 3:14)
Walking in Love (Eph. 5:2)
Standing in Armor (Eph. 6:13)

374 Threefold Judgment

As Sinners (Gal. 2:20; John 5:24)—Past
As Saints (1 Cor. 11:31, 32; 1 Peter 5:19)—Present
As Servants (2 Cor. 5:9; 1 Cor. 3:13-15)—Future

375   Boldness

Boldness to draw near to God (Heb. 10:19)
Boldness to speak the Word (Acts 6:31)
Boldness in the Judgment (1 John 4:17)

376   Three Divine Provisions
For all the Lord's People

The *Will* of the Lord (James 5:14)—Our Guide
The *Way* of the Lord (Acts 18:25)—Our Path
The *Work* of the Lord (1 Cor. 15:58)—Our Business

377   Things We Are to "Find"

Rest under the Yoke *of* Christ (Matt. 11:29)
Pasture by going in and out *with* Christ (John 10:9)
Grace by drawing near *to* Christ (Heb. 4:16)

378   Angelic Joy

At Creation (Job 27:7)
At Incarnation (Luke 2:13)
At Conversion (Luke 15:10)

379   The Believer's Body

A *Member* of Christ (1 Cor. 6:15)
A *Temple* of the Spirit (1 Cor. 6:19)
A *Sacrifice* to God (Rom. 12:1)

380   The Believer in Three Relations

Upright in his relation to God (Prov. 14:2)
Unspotted in his relation to the World (James 1:27)
Unblameable in his relation to the Church (1 Thess. 2:10)

381 A Busy Chapter
(Acts 12)

Persecution of the Saints (vv. 1-4)
Prison for the Servant (vv. 5-11)
Prayer of the Church (vv. 12-17)
Preservation by the Lord (vv. 17-23)
Progress of the Word (v. 24)
Pride and its Punishment (vv. 21-23)

382 Bible Houses

House of Bondage (Deut. 7:8; 8:14)
House of Salvation (Exod. 12:7, 13, 27)
House of Instruction (Deut. 6:7; 11:19)
House of Communion (Song of Sol. 2:4; Ps. 84:4)
House of Reunion (John 14:2)

383 Four Cardinal Truths

Redemption (Eph. 1:7)—For the Slave
Reconciliation (Rom. 5:10)—For the Enemy
Regeneration (Titus 3:5)—For the Sinner
Restoration (Gal. 6:1)—For the Wanderer

384 What We Wait for

Waiting for the Coming of the Lord (1 Cor. 1:7)
Waiting for the Redemption of the Body (Rom. 8:23)
Waiting for the Manifestation of the Sons of God (Rom. 8:19)

385 Effectual Prayer

In the Name of Christ (John 14:13-14)
In the Holy Ghost (Jude 20)
In Faith (James 1:6; Heb. 11:6)

386   Light

Our Enlightenment (2 Cor. 4:6)—Light in us
Our Environment (1 Peter 2:9)—We into light
Our Employment (Eph. 5:8)—Walk in light
Our Equipment (Rom. 13:12)—Armor of light

387ᐟ   Laying On of Hands

In Blessings (Gen. 48:14-20; Mark 10:16)
In Judgment (Lev. 24:15; Deut. 17:7)
In Impartation (Acts 8:17; 19:6)
In Fellowship (Acts 13:3)

388   The Rock

Of Salvation (2 Sam. 22:47)
Of Shelter (Ps. 61:2)
Of Refreshment (1 Cor. 10:4)

389   Three Remarkable Days

Day of Salvation (2 Cor. 6:2)
Day of Redemption (Eph. 4:30)
Day of Judgment (2 Peter 2:9)

390   Good Security

"*No* weapon formed against you shall prosper" (Isa. 54:17)
"*Nothing* shall by any means hurt you" (Luke 10:19)
"*No one* is able to pluck you" (John 10:28)

391   Prayer

Personal (Eph. 1:16; 3:14)
Social (Acts 12:12)
Church (Acts 2:42; 12:5)

392 Pride

Pride of Race (John 8:33)—National
Pride of Place (James 2:2-3)—Social
Pride of Face (James 1:24)—Personal
Pride of Grace (1 Tim. 6:4)—Spiritual

393 John's Four Sights of Christ

"We beheld His glory" (John 1:14)

At the Transfiguration (Mark 9:7)
At the Crucifixion (John 19:26)
At the Resurrection (John 21:20)
In the Revelation (Rev. 1:16-17)

394 "Take Heed"

"What ye hear" (Mark 4:24)—The Matter
"How ye hear" (Luke 8:18)—The Manner
"How you build" (1 Cor. 3:10)—The Work

395 Three "Walks"

Our Old Walk (Eph. 2:3)—Past
Our New Walk (Rom. 6:4)—Present
Our Future Walk (Rev. 3:4)—Prospective

396 Three Seals

The Father's Seal on the Son (John 6:37)
The Believer's Seal on the Word (John 3:33)
The Spirit's Seal on the Saint (Eph. 1:13)

397 Giving

God gave His Son (John 3:16)
Christ gave Himself (Gal. 2:20)
Believers give themselves (2 Cor. 8:5)

398   The Faithfulness of God

In Cleansing from Sin (1 John 1:9)
In Delivering from Temptation (1 Cor. 10:13)
In Keeping from Evil (2 Thess. 3:3)
In Sanctifying Wholly (1 Thess. 5:24)

399   "Striving"

The word in all these texts is the same throughout, and
    might be uniformly translated "agonize"

In Prayer (Col. 4:12)
In Conflict (2 Tim. 4:7)
In Ministry (Col. 1:29)
In Running (1 Cor. 9:25)

400   "With One Accord"

In Prayer (Acts 1:14; 4:24)
In Hearing the Word (Acts 8:6)
In Gathering together (Acts 2:46; 5:12)
In Peace and Unity (Acts 15:25)

401   Things to "Buy"

Wine and milk (Isa. 55:1)—For Salvation
The Truth (Prov. 23:23)—For Sanctification
Gold tried in the fire (Rev. 3:18)—For Preservation

402   "I Come Quickly"

Three times in Revelation 22

"I come quickly" (v. 7)—To the Disciple
"I come quickly" (v. 12)—To the Servant
"I come quickly" (v. 20)—To the Bride

403   Warning Words

Beware of Covetousness (Luke 12:15)—The Heart
Beware of Men (Col. 2:8)—The Mind
Beware of False Teachers (2 Peter 3:17)—The Path

404   Three Looks

Looking *to* the Savior (Isa. 45:22)—Salvation
Looking *on* the Master (John 1:36)—Contemplation
Looking *for* the Bridegroom (Titus 2:13)—Glorification

405   Baptismal Truths

The Baptism of John (Matt. 3:6)—Repentance
The Baptism of the Cross (Luke 12:50)—Judgment
The Baptism of the Spirit (1 Cor. 12:13)—Unity
The Baptism of Believers (Rom. 6:4)—Identification

406   Baptism

Believers are the Subjects (Acts 6:41; 8:12)
Immersion is the Mode (Matt. 3:16; Acts 8:38)
Burial is the Meaning (Rom. 6:4; Col. 2:12)

407   The Lord's Supper

Its Institution (Matt. 26:26-28)
Its Celebration (Acts 20:7; 1 Cor. 11:23)
Its Meaning (1 Cor. 10:16; 11:24-26)

CHURCH TRUTHS

408   Two Aspects of the Church

The Body of Christ (1 Cor. 12:12-13)—Of Living Members
The Temple of God (1 Peter 2:5)—Of Living Stones

Christ is *Head* over the Body
Christ is *Foundation* of the Temple

409   The Church Locally

Composed of Believers (1 Cor. 1-2; 1 Thess. 1:1-9)
Gathered unto the Name (Matt. 18:20; 1 Cor. 5:4)
Governed by the Lord (1 Cor. 12:3-5)
Guided by the Spirit (1 Cor. 12:7-8; Phil. 3:3)
Ordered by the Word (1 Cor. 11:23; 12:36-37)

410   The Church's Constitution

(Matthew 18:20)

"Where"—A Divine Location
"Two or three"—A Divine Testimony
"Are Gathered"—A Divine Drawing
"Together"—A Divine Unity
"In My Name"—A Divine Authority
"There am I"—The Divine Presence
"In the midst of them"—The Divine Center

411 "Churches of the Saints"

Composed of Saints by Calling (Rom. 1:7; Eph. 1:1)
Commended by Saintly Character (Philem. 1:5-17; Rom. 16:2)
Characterized by Saintly Conduct (Rom. 12:13; Eph. 5:3; Heb. 6:10)
Constituted by Faith delivered to the Saints (Jude 3)

412 The Church Prospectively

A Mystery to be Revealed (Eph. 3:3-9)
A Pearl to be Purchased (Matt. 13:45-46)
A Building to be Begun (Matt. 16:17-18)

413 Four Figures of the Church

A House for God (1 Tim. 3)—To Rule
A Body for Christ (Eph. 1:23)—To Supply
A Temple for the Spirit (Eph. 2)—To Indwell
A Lampstand to the World (Rev. 2; 3)—To Give Light

414 The Church in Four Epochs

In the Purpose of God (Eph. 1:4; Titus 1:2)
Purchased at the Cross (Eph. 5:26; Acts 20:28)
Formed by the Spirit (1 Cor. 12:13; Eph. 4:4)
Presented in Glory (Eph. 5:27; Jude 24)

415 The Church at Ephesus

Its Formation (Acts 18:9)
Its Instruction (Eph. 1—6)
Its Watching (1 Tim. 1:3)
Its Danger (Acts 20:17-29)
Its Inspection (Rev. 1:13; 2:1-7)

416 The Church's Pattern

The Master Builder's Instructions (1 Cor. 3:10; 11:1)
The Architect's Pattern (1 Cor. 11:2, 23; 1 Tim. 3:15)
The Proper Materials (1 Cor. 3:12; 1 Peter 2:5)
The Way to Build (Eph. 4:12; Phil. 2:1)

417 Receiving to Church Fellowship

Whom to Receive—"Saints" (Rom. 14:1; Matt. 18:5)
How to Receive—"in the Lord" (Rom. 16:2; Philem. 15-17;
   Phil. 2:29)
Who are to Receive?—"Ye" (Rom. 15:6-7)
To What are they Received?—"The Fellowship" (Acts
   2:42-44; 9:28)
Whom to Avoid (Rom. 16:18; Titus 3:10; 2 Tim. 3:5)

418 A Good Church Condition

As seen in Acts 9:31

Rest from persecution or strife outwardly (1 Cor. 14:33)
Edification, built up, inwardly (Eph. 4:16)
Ministry, in the Spirit unhindered
Walk, in the fear of the Lord
Multiplication, growth from within

419 Seven Links of Fellowship

Gathered Together (Matt. 18:20)
Framed Together (Eph. 2:21)
Builded Together (Eph. 2:22)
Knit Together (Col. 2:2)
Perfectly joined Together (1 Cor. 1:10)
Striving Together (Phil. 1:27)
Caught up Together (1 Thess. 4:17)

420   The Church Corrupted

From Within by	*From Without* by
Evil Doctrine (1 Tim. 1:20)	Unconverted Professors (Jude 4)
Perverse Things (Acts 20:30)	False Teachers (2 Peter 2:1)
False Brethren (Gal. 2:4)	Many Antichrists (1 John 2:18)
Proud Men (John 3:9)	Fables Taught (2 Tim. 4:4)
Indifference (Rev. 2:20)	Amalgamation with World (Rev. 2:13)

421   Seven Fellowships

Fellowship with the Father (1 John 1:3)
Fellowship of the Son (1 Cor. 1:9)
Fellowship of the Spirit (Phil. 2:1)
Fellowship in the Light (1 John 1:7)
Fellowship of Suffering (Phil. 3:10)
Fellowship in Service (Col. 4:7)
Fellowship in the Gospel (Phil. 1:3)

422   The Seven Churches

A History of the entire Church through the age
(Revelation 2 and 3)

Ephesus, the Church in early purity
Smyrna, the Church in Persecution
Pergamos, the Church united with the World
Thyatira, Romanism ruling supreme
Sardis, Protestantism
Philadelphia, the Faithful few
Laodicea, the World-church

The last four go on together until the end

423   Worship and Worshippers

What Worship is (Matt. 2:11; 28:9; 1 Cor. 14:25)
Who are Worshipers (John 4:23; 1 Peter 2:9; Phil. 3:3)
The Place of Worship (Heb. 9:20; Eph. 2:18)
The Power for Worship (Phil. 3:3; John 4:24)

Worship ascends from saints, *in* the Spirit, *through* Christ, *to* the Father.

424   Ministry

Christ Glorified (Eph. 4:8-11)—Its Source
The Spirit (1 Cor. 12:4)—Its Administrator
Edification (Eph. 4:11)—Its Object

Ministry comes *from* God, *through* Christ, *in* the Spirit, *to* the Church.

425   Rule

The Holy Spirit, the Creator of it (Acts 20:28)
The Marks of True Rulers (1 Tim. 3:1-7)
The Duty of owning them (1 Thess. 5:12)

426   Discipline

Its Necessity and Object (1 Tim. 5:20)
Its Internal Form (2 Thess. 3:6-14)
Its Extreme Measure (1 Cor. 5:11-13)
Its Object, Restoration (2 Cor. 2:7)

427   Fellowship of Churches

In Mutual Recognition (Acts 18:27; Rom. 16:1)
In Service and toward Servants (Acts 11:22; 13:3)
In Substance and Suffering (2 Cor. 8:1; Acts 11:29)

SCRIPTURE TEXT TOPICS

428   The Great Deliverance
(Galatians 1:3-4)

The Giver—"Our Lord Jesus Christ"
The Gift—"Himself"
The Object—"For *our* Sins"
The End—"Deliverance from the World"

429   Asa's Prayer
(2 Chronicles 14:11)

It was Earnest—"He Cried"
It was Personal—"To God"
It was Definite—"Help us"
It was Believing—"We rest on Thee"
It was Answered—Verses 12-15

430   The Believer's History
(Deuteronomy 32:10)

"Found," with Luke 15:4-5—A Lost Sinner
"Led," with John 10:4-28—A Loving Follower
"Instructed," with Luke 10:39—A Lowly Disciple
"Kept," with 1 Peter 1:5—A Living Saint

431 The Exaltation of Christ
(Isaiah 52:13-15)

"Exalted"—At His Ascension (Acts 2:33; 5:31)
"Extolled"—In His Glory (Rev. 4:11; 5:12-14)
"Very High"—In His Kingdom (Rev. 19:16)
All the words in the Hebrew, signify majesty and power

432 Faithful Witnesses in Difficult Places

Noah in a godless World (2 Peter 2:5)
Joseph, in an Officer's House (Gen. 39:2-9)
David, in a King's Palace (1 Sam. 16:14-23)
Daniel, in a Heathen Court (Dan. 1:8)
Mordecai, in an Enemy's Presence (Esth. 2:1-6)

433 The Footsteps of the Flock
(Song of Solomon 1:7-8)

An Appeal to the Shepherd (Isa. 40:11)
Rested Flock (Ps. 23:2; Jer. 6:16)
Rival Shepherds (1 Cor. 1:12-13; 3:4-6)
A Gracious Answer (Ps. 25:9; 27:9)
A Plain Path (Acts 2:41-47)
Feeding and Leading (John 21:15; 1 Peter 5:2)

434 Burden Bearing
(Galatians 6:2-5)

"Bear one another's burdens" (v. 2)

Sharing in sorrow, in sympathy, in trial—Fellowship of saints.

"Every man shall bear his own burden" (v. 5)

Personal and individual responsibility, which must be borne by each, like a ship bringing its cargo into port—Individual Responsibility.

435 Weary and Unweary

(Isaiah 40:28-31)

The Unfailing and Unwearying God (v. 29)
Fainting and Wearying Man (v. 30)
The Waiting Soul Renewed (v. 31)
Strength Imparted to Mount up (v. 31)
Run unwearied, Walk unfainting (v. 31)

436 Benjamin's Blessing

(Deuteronomy 32:12)

True of all the Lord's "little ones" (Gen. 44:20)
"The Beloved of the Lord" (Rom. 1:7; Col. 3:12)
"Dwell in safety, by Him" (Ps. 91:1; Acts 11:23)
"Cover him all day long" (Ps. 91:4; 84:11)
"Dwell between His shoulders" (1 Peter 1:5; Jude 24)

437 Downward and Upward

(Isaiah 37:31)

"Root Downward"—The Hidden Life, as set forth in Ps. 1:3;
   Jer. 17:7-8; John 15:1-6; Jude 21
"Fruit Upward"—The Manifested Life as described in Rom.
   7:4; Eph. 5:9; Gal. 5:22; Rom. 6:22; Phil. 1:11

PROPHETIC THEMES

438　The Personal Return of Christ

The Lord's own Promise (John 14:3, with Heb. 10:36-37)
A Personal Return (Acts 1:11, with Rev. 22:12)
The Lord Himself (1 Thess. 4:16; Rev. 22:17)
The Christian's Hope (1 Tim. 1:1; 1 John 3:3)

439　The Believer's Attitude

Waiting for His Coming (1 Cor. 1:7; 1 Thess. 1:10)
Looking for that Blessed Hope (Titus 2:13; Phil. 3:20)
The Sleeping Saints, with Christ (Phil. 1:23; 2 Cor. 5:8)
The Living Saints waiting for Christ (Rev. 22:20)
Its Practical Power (1 John 3:3; 1 Thess. 3:13)

440　Christ's Coming for His Saints

The Lord Descends to the Air (1 Thess. 4:16)
The Dead in Christ are Raised (1 Cor. 15:20-25)
The Living Saints are Changed (1 Thess. 4:17)
Incorruptibility given the Dead (1 Cor. 15:52)
Immortality given to the Living (1 Cor. 15:54)
Caught up Together (1 Thess. 4:17)
Received by Him (John 14:3)

441　The Gathering and Presentation

Gathered Together unto Him (2 Thess. 2:1)
Welcomed to the Father's House (John 14:2; 17:24)
Presented, the Church Glorious (Eph. 5:27)
Presented faultless in glory (Jude 24)
Crowned in Heaven (Rev. 4:4-10; 5:6-9)

442   The Judgment Seat of Christ

The Master's Promise (Rev. 22:12; Luke 19:13)
The Reckoning Day (Matt. 25:19; 1 Cor. 4:5)
The Manifestation of Works (2 Cor. 5:10; Col. 3:24-25)
Motives and Manner (1 Cor. 4:5; 2 Tim. 2:5)
Reward and Loss (1 Cor. 3:13; 9:24-26)
Crowns and Castaways (2 Tim. 4:8; 1 Peter 5:4)

443   The Marriage of the Lamb

A Scene in Heaven (Rev. 19:7)
The Bride Prepared (Rev. 19:7; 2 Cor. 11:2)
The Guests Invited (Rev. 19:9, with John 3:29)
The Joy in Heaven (Rev. 19:7; Jude 24)
The Bride's Attire (Rev. 19:8)

444   The Manifestation in Glory

Called the "Appearing" or "Epiphany"

To be distinguished from the *Parousia*, or "Coming"
The Manifestation of Christ in Glory (Titus 2:13)
With all His Saints (Col. 3:4; Rev. 19:11-16)
In Public Glory (Matt. 24:30; Rom. 8:19)
To Overthrow His Foes (2 Thess. 1:7-10; Jude 14)
To Establish His Kingdom (Zech 14:4-9; Matt. 17:4)

445   The Day of the Lord

A Period of Judgment (Isa. 2:12-21; 2 Peter 3:10)
It will come suddenly (1 Thess. 5:2; Rev. 3:3)
Judgment on Christ rejecters (2 Thess. 1:8-10; 2:7-12)
Destruction of Antichrist (2 Thess. 2:6-8; Rev. 19:20)
Judgment of Apostate Christianity (Rev. 17 and 18)
Satan cast into the Abyss (Rev. 20:3)

446   Restoration of Israel

The Promises of God (Rom. 11:26; Isa. 11:11-12)
Conviction and Conversion (Zech. 12:9-14; 13:1)
Return to their Land (Isa. 11:12; 14:1-2; Amos 9:9)
Reunion of the Tribes (Ezek. 20:33-38; Isa. 46:20)
The Earthly City (Ps. 48:2; 122:1; Zech. 14:8)
The Center of Government (Mic. 4:2; Jer. 33:16)

447   The Millennium

The Reign of Christ Predicted (Isa. 32:1; Luke 1:32)
Its Postponement (Luke 19:14; Matt. 23:38-39)
Its Certain Fulfilment (Ps. 72:1; Heb. 1:8)
Its Characteristics (Isa. 11 and 35; Rev. 20:6)
Its Blessings (Ps. 72:5-8; Isa. 2:4)
Its Heavenly Sphere (Rev. 20:4; 21:10-27)
Its Earthly Aspect (Rom. 8:20-21; Isa. 11:9)

448   The Final Judgment

Satan Loosed (Rev. 20:7-8). His Doom (Rev. 20:10)
The Last Great Rebellion (Rev. 20:9-27)
The Heavens and Earth Pass Away (2 Peter 3:10)
The Dead are Raised (John 5:25-29; Rev. 20:12)
The Judge on the Throne (Rev. 20:11; Acts 17:31)
The Open Books (Rev. 20:12; Rom. 2:16; Rev. 3:5)
The Final Doom (Rev. 20:15; 21:8; Mark 9:48)

449   The Eternal State

A New Heaven and Earth (Rev. 21:1-5; 2 Peter 3:13)
The New Jerusalem (Rev. 21:1-4; 22:1-5)
The Eternal Glory of Christ and His People (1 Peter 5:10)
God Dwelling with Men (Rev. 21:3; Eph. 2:21)
God, "All in All" (1 Cor. 15:25)

BIBLE STUDIES

450   Life, Light, Liberty

The Word received gives *Life* (John 5:24)
The Word entering gives *Light* (Ps. 119:108)
The Truth known gives *Liberty* (John 8:32)

451   God's Joy

In His People's Salvation (Luke 15:24)
In His People's Obedience (3 John 4)
In His People's Glorification (Jude 24)

452   The Two Natures

The Old (Rom. 7:18; 8:18; Eph. 4:22)
The New (1 John 3:9; Eph. 4:26)
The Conflict (Gal. 5:17; Rom. 7:25)
The Way of Victory (Rom. 8:2-13; Gal. 5:16-25)

453   Gospel Service

In Three Aspects

"Trustees" (1 Thess. 2:4)—To guard it
"Stewards" (1 Cor. 9:7)—To Administer it
"Ambassadors" (2 Cor. 5:20)—To Present it

454   A Threefold Ministry

Ministers of God (2 Cor.6:4; 1 Thess. 3:2)
Ministers of Christ (2 Cor. 11:23; Col. 1:7)
Ministers of the Word (Acts 6:4; 2 Tim. 4:4)

455   Key Words in Ephesians

"In Christ" (Eph. 1:3)—Standing
"In the Lord" (Eph. 6:1)—Subjection
"In the Spirit" (Eph. 5:18)—Condition
"In one Body" (Eph. 2:16)—Unity

456   Lamps and Light

As a Candle in the Home (Luke 11:33-36)
As a Lamp in the Church (Rev. 1:12)*
As a Star in the World (Rev. 1:16; 2:1-20)

   *The word here is Lampstand (not Candlestick). Believers are the
Lamps; the Church, the Lampstand.

457   A Threefold Possession
(1 Corinthians 3:22-23)

"All are your's" (Eph. 1:3; Rom. 8:32; 1 Tim. 6:17)
"Ye are Christ's" (1 Cor. 6:20; Mark 9:41)
"Christ is God's" (Matt. 3:17; Heb. 1:5; Ps. 2:7)

458   The Great Commission
(Matthew 28:18-20)

The Master's Authority (v. 18, with John 17:2)
The Servant's Commission (v. 19, with Mark 15:15)
The Making of Disciples (v. 19, with Acts 14:21)
The Baptizing of them (v. 19, with Acts 10:48)
Teaching them all things (v. 20, with Acts 14:28)
The Promised Presence (v. 20, with Acts 11:21)

459   Words to Shepherds
(1 Thessalonians 5:12-14)

A Threefold Work among the Healthy (v. 12)
Three Classes of Lame and Feeble (v. 14)
A Threefold Service toward such (v. 14)

460   Four "Alls"

(Matthew 28:18-20)

"All Authority" given to the Lord Jesus
"All Nations," to be Evangelized
"All Things," to be taught Disciples
"All the Days," the Lord's Presence Promised

461   A Triple Glory of Christ

(Revelation 1:5)

The Faithful Witness: Incarnate on Earth—Past
The First Begotten: Glorified in Heaven—Present
The Prince of Kings: Reigning overall—Future

462   A Threefold Exhortation

(Hebrews 10:19-24)

"Let us draw near" (v. 22)—Faith's Exercise
"Let us hold fast" (v. 23)—Hope's Grasp
"Let us consider" (v. 24)—Love's Labor

463   Followers or "Imitators"

(1 Thessalonians)

Followers of us and the Lord (1 Thess. 1:4)—Individual
Followers of Churches of God (1 Thess. 2:14)—Corporate
The Gospel believed, produced the former (1:4)
The Word received, effected the latter (2:13)

464   Three Stages in Christ's Path

(Philippians 2:6-11)

From the Bosom of the Father to Bethlehem (vv. 6-7)
From the Manger to the Cross (vv. 7-8)
From the Grave to the Throne (vv. 9-11)

465   Two Aspects of Christian Life

A Man in Christ (2 Cor. 12:1)—Standing
Christ in Regenerate Man (2 Cor. 13:5)—State

466   Two Scenes in Luke's Gospel

It opens with the Earthly Priest at the altar of incense on
   earth, and the people worshiping without, in doubt
   and fear (Luke 1:8-21).
It closes with the Great High Priest entering the Heavenly
   Temple, and His saints worshiping with great joy
   (Luke 24:50-53).

467   Mansions or "Abodes"

(John 14)

Mansions awaiting Saints in God's Heaven (v. 2)
Mansions for God with Saints on earth (v. 23)
The word in the original is the same in both verses

468   Young Men of the Bible

Patterns to Young Men in all ages

Moses left all, in Faith (Heb. 11:24)
Joseph endured all, in Hope (Gen. 45:5)
Jonathan surrendered all, in Love (1 Sam. 18:4)
Daniel triumphed over all, in Obedience (Dan. 1:6)

469   Young Women of the Bible

Bright Examples of Devotion

Rebekah left all for Isaac (Gen. 24:58)
Ruth found all in Bethlehem (Ruth 2:12)
Esther risked all for her people (Esther 4:16)

470   Two Characteristics of this Age

The *Ascent* of the Son to the Throne (Acts 1)
The *Descent* of the Spirit to the World (Acts 2)

471   Three Classes

(1 Corinthians 10:32)

"The Jew;" The National—Religious
"The Gentile;" The Heathen—Idolatrous
"The Church of God;" The Spiritual—Christians

472   Eternal Life

Promised by God (Titus 1:4)—Its Source
Ever in Christ (John 1:4)—Its Spring
Manifested by Christ (1 John 1:2)—Its Stream
Given through Christ (Rom. 6:23)—Its Channel
Hid with Christ (Col. 3:3)—Its Security
Possessed by Believers (1 John 5:9)—A Present Enjoyment
Hoped for in Fruition (Titus 1:2)—A Future Hope

473   Lawlessness

In its nature insubordinate to God and His Word

"Sin in Lawlessness" (1 John 3:4)
The Natural Condition of all (Rom. 8:7; Job 11:12)
Religious Profession Covers (Matt. 23:7; 2 Tim. 3:5)
Hated by the Lord Jesus (Heb. 1:9)
Redemption Delivers from it (Titus 2:14)

474   Jesus Christ, Our Shepherd

The Good Shepherd (John 10:11)—Died to Save us
The Great Shepherd (Heb. 13:20)—Lives to Guide us
The Chief Shepherd (1 Peter 5:3)—Comes to Glorify us

475   Preaching in Acts 10

Preaching Peace through His Blood (v. 36)
Proclaiming Forgiveness in His Name (v. 44)
Announcing Judgment on the Impenitent (v. 42)

476   Good Spiritual Condition

Full of the Holy Ghost and Faith—Barnabas (Acts 11:24)
Full of Faith and Power—Stephen (Acts 6:8)
Full of Good Works and Alms Deed—Dorcas (Acts 9:36)

477   Seven Steps in Peter's Fall

1. Doubts (Matt. 14:28, with 16:23)
2. Boasts (Mark 14:27-31, with 1 Cor. 10:12)
3. Sleeps (Mark 14:37, with Rom. 13:11)
4. Smites (John 18:10, with Luke 22:50)
5. Follows afar off (Luke 22:54)
6. Sits with the Ungodly (Luke 22:55)
7. Denies the Lord (Luke 22:57-62)

478 Seven Steps in Peter's Restoration

1. The Lord's Prayer and Look (Luke 22:32-61)
2. Peter's Conviction, Tears, Repentance (Luke 22:61-62)
3. Hears and Hastens to the Sepulcher (John 20:1-4)
4. Receives a Message from the Lord (Mark 16:7)
5. Private Meeting with the Lord (Luke 24:34)
6. Public Restoration to Service (John 21:15-17)
7. Boldly Testifies for Christ (Acts 3:14)

CHRISTIAN SERVICE

479   Willing and Wise
A Willing Heart to Give (Exod. 35:5)—To God
A Wise Heart to Work (Exod. 35:10)—For God

480   Behind and Before
"Forgetting"—the things that are behind
"Forth-reaching"—to the glories that are before

481   Lord and Master
(Acts 27:23)
"Whose I am"—Christ my Owner
"Whom I serve"—Christ my Master

482   Three Conditions of Soul
"Cast Down" (2 Cor. 7:6)—By Discouragement
"Puffed Up" (Col. 2:18)—In Pride
"Pressing On" (Phil. 3:14)—By Faith

483   Credentials for Service
Gift from God (Eph. 4:8; 1 Peter 4:16)
Grace to use it to God (Eph. 4:7; Rom. 12:3)
Godliness to command it for God (1 Tim. 4:7)

484   A Threefold Service
(Jude 20, 21)
"*Building* up yourselves" (v. 20)—The Word
"*Praying* in the Holy Spirit" (v. 20)—The Throne
"*Looking* for the mercy of our Lord" (v. 21)—The Hope

485   A Triple Employment
Pray Unceasingly (1 Thess. 5:17; Eph. 6:18)
Praise Unflaggingly (Eph. 5:19-20; Heb. 13:15)
Preach Unweariedly (2 Tim. 4:2; 1 Cor. 15:58)

486 Our Work in Three Aspects
Workers for His Name (3 John 7)
Witnesses for His Truth (Acts 1:8)
Watchers for His Coming (Mark 13:35)

487 A Threefold Working
The Lord working *for* us (John 17:4)
The Lord working *in* us (Heb. 13:21)
The Lord working *with* us (Mark 16:20)

488 Our Stewardship
A Steward of God (Titus 1:7)—A High Honor
A Good Steward (1 Peter 4:10)—A Great Trust
A Faithful Steward (1 Cor. 4:2)—A Noble Aim
A Wise Steward (Luke 12:42)—A Discerning Mind
An Unjust Steward (Luke 16:2)—A Selfish Motive

489 Badges of Christian Service
Holiness (1 Thess. 2:10, with Luke 1:75)
Humility (Acts 20:19, with James 4:6)
Hope (1 Cor. 9:9, with James 5:7)

490 Bugle Calls to Servants
"Holding *faith* and a good conscience" (1 Tim. 1:19)
"Holding *fast* the faithful Word" (Titus 1:9)
"Holding *forth* the Word of Life" (Phil. 2:12)

491 Fellowship in Service
One Will (1 Cor. 4:19; James 4:15)
One Walk (1 Cor. 4:17; 2 Cor. 12:18)
One Work (1 Cor. 16:10; 16:21)

492 Enoch, an Old-Time Witness
His faith *in* God (Heb. 11:5)
His walk *with* God (Gen. 5:24)
His testimony *for* God (Jude 14)

493   Two Causes of Unfruitfulness
"They had no root" (Matt. 13:6)—Christless
"It lacked moisture" (Luke 8:6)—Spiritless

494   Walk and Work
Walking with God (Gen. 5:24)—One Path
Working with God (1 Sam. 14:45)—One Object

495   Good Employment
Always Praying (Phil. 1:4)—In the Spirit
Always Rejoicing (2 Cor. 6:10)—In the Lord
Always Abounding (1 Cor. 15:58)—In the Work

496   The Gospeller
Saved by the Gospel (2 Tim. 1:8-9)—Conversion
Separated to the Gospel (Rom. 1:1)—Consecration
Sent with the Gospel (Acts 13:4)—Commission

497   Spiritual Outfit
Shod to walk (Deut. 33:25, with Eph. 6:15)
Girded to Serve (Ps. 18:32, with John 13:4)
Armed to Fight (Eph. 6:10, with 1 Tim. 6:12)

498   Paul's Preaching
(Acts 20:24-28)
The Gospel of the grace of God (v. 24)—The Message
The Kingdom of God (v. 25)—The Object
The Counsel of God (v. 27)—The Instrument

499   Watchwords of Service
"*Hitherto* hath the Lord helped us" (1 Sam. 7:12)
"*Henceforth* live...unto Him" (2 Cor. 5:13)

500   "With Christ"
In Life (Eph. 2:5)
In Suffering (2 Tim. 2:17)
In Glory (John 17:34)

INDEX

No.

128 / Index